Here I Still Am

Here I Still Am

Poems

Larry D. Quillian

Library of Congress Control Number: 2020921630
ISBN: Hardcover   978-1-6641-4007-3
               Softcover   978-1-6641-4008-0
               eBook   978-1-6641-4009-7

Scripture quotations marked KJV are from the Holy Bible, King James Version (Authorized Version). First published in 1611. Quoted from the KJV Classic Reference Bible, Copyright © 1983 by The Zondervan Corporation.

Any people depicted in stock imagery provided by Getty Images are models, and such images are being used for illustrative purposes only.
Certain stock imagery © Getty Images.

Print information available on the last page.

Rev. date: 11/23/2020

To order additional copies of this book, contact:
Xlibris
844-714-8691
www.Xlibris.com
Orders@Xlibris.com
821995

Introduction

In my first two poetry books, **A Peek Inside** and **Burn Before Reading**, I tried to touch on everything, lightly. My intent in this book, **Here I Still Am**, is to dig a bit deeper into subjects that interest me. So, don't be surprised at more inconsistencies. My hope is that these poems make you stop and think, even more.

Ldq

He Puzzles, Still!

Seeking knowledge/wisdom, always,
    this child of man puzzled away his life.
He had had but one life-time to learn
    that true beauty is expressed in love…
And *that* truth—and truth itself—
    had…has alluded him:
Why life, if not for purpose?
    Reality cried out the question: *why?*
And, now, at his end-time,
    the question has morphed to: *Why not?*
And *as* answer: *No* answer is there.
    And *he puzzles, still!*

Dedication

I dedicate this book to all of my fellow existentialist who, like me, are hoping against what they/we know that they/we are wrong, and that the world is somehow full of sentient souls who will all find and spend an eternity together.

And good luck with that, guys!

ldq

Here I Still Am

Here I still am, in my eternity of words,
    speaking, forever,
To a reader—any reader—any mind
    who has opened these pages of mine:
My poems, my thoughts…my words,
    all that I ever was, *here I still am*.

Contents

Love Song To The World

Speck in a huge and expanding galaxy,
    that is a speck in endless reality,
that is so close to being nothing at all
    that we have yet to be noticed by:
What? if *what* is the answer:
    by *that* light or *that* dark,
By anything that can notice,
    by, *we will call this mystery: God.*
Yet womb to life, to man,
    mother of life that's known,
The only source of understanding
    that *might* be felt in the bowels
of black holes, you, giver and maker
    and home to *all known* life,
You, World, are my only possibility for love....
    So, please, *please* sing with me now, *World,*
Sing with me now that we are in synergy,
    now that I have pledged my life to you.
Such is my need to hear your voice, your song,
    that I will say, *yes,* to all you ask.

I Had A Dream

I had a dream
    that, somewhere,
In the immensity of the universe,
    life evolved
Feeding on *non-organic* matter,
    and that intelligent beings evolved
Without the need to cannibalize
    other life.
I had a dream that evolution
    was benign to life,
And, that nothing that lived,
    killed,
Not for need! Not for pleasure!
    Not for sport!
That intelligence evolved
    believing in
The utter uniqueness of life,
    and that life was
Totally sacrosanct
    and that *all* assets
Were communal
    and that *all* pain
Was empathetically shared.
    I had a dream….

Immortality?

Straining against the truth of life:
    Knowing and not knowing,
Believing and not believing,
    cursing and praying.
We want to know—and we know—
    but we can't accept the truth…
Something inside of us
    just will not let us die!
And so we create immortality
    and live for tomorrow instead of today.
Seven billion plus of us and counting,
    nuclear energy and space exploration,
Medicine that threatens disease in every form:
    bacterial, viral, genetic—even ageing;
Architecture, art, public works;
    food for everyone,
And the rivers run
    where *we* say.
What is matter, life, consciousness?
    We think we'll know—and we might.
Then what—so what—
    that nagging problem still:
Immortality!
    We know we made it up—*but still.…*
Our biological imperative is to be immortal.
    God, it seems, is inherent in our genes.

I Hope To Dream

Out of the wilderness of sleep
    I come prancing,
Glad to escape the inconsistent
    life of sleep,
Where happenings are bizarre,
    unpredictable
And out of conscious control,
    out of reasoned predictability,
Yet often full of meaning
    that is, sometimes, instructive.
Mysteries, then, to be quickly forgotten
    or to disturb for days, months—*or years....*
Who would sleep on purpose,
    but one dissatisfied with their days?
Who would enter, nightly,
    mysterious events
That, often, demand examination,
    that seem to tell a familiar story,
That *must* mean something,
    but that are mostly ghostly thoughts?
Sleep *has* to mean something!
    It is too graphic to dismiss,
Yet, too whimsical to believe,
    too illogical to live in while awake.
Perhaps, another life for the dreamer...
    perhaps, a necessary fulfillment
Of need...or desire...or fear...
    impossible! so, paroled on waking.
And, again, tonight, *I hope to dream,*
    again, and again and again.

Math

When AI speaks for the universe—
    Artificial Intelligence for the physical—
Life will still live for life,
    and Man will speak for the living.
We are to be contested by our own creation:
    AI is the end product of *Man's* handiwork,
The offspring of biology,
    and the future of the universe,
(And, maybe, its past...)
    but Man has broken into the answer:
It has taken biology to step ahead,
    to supply the necessary hands
To make, build, create
    God in the form of Creator.
Life may have been a fluke, a chemical accident,
    while the future of the universe
Was found hiding in a mathematic formula....
    So, it looks like God may be *math*.

3 a. m.

It's *3 a.m.* and I'm awake, *again,*
    to face the truth—oh God—*and me.*
I'm not and will not be immortal:
    Reason shouts that that is so.
There's no more sleeping from the truth
    when you're awake at *3 a.m.*
Most all the beings that I know,
    that I still see in memory,
Are dead
    and gone from touch and call...
Yet still they're drifting—sifting through
    my mind at night, at *3 a.m.*
They come and go as though at will—
    not called—just *come and go....*
Their words and faces fill my thoughts
    as vividly they come and go.
No thing has changed inside my head,
    except, of course, I know they're dead,
Yet still they're here and real to me
    as when I called them on the phone,
Or walked them home,
    or touched their hands...or lips....
But will they stay when I am dead,
    will they stay inside my head?
And where was I before my birth?
    I go there soon, to meet...with, whom?
The universe I know is real,
    And what I know must end with me.
At core the atom's made of strings;
    vibration sets each one apart.

Apart, one particle exists:
    one entity both here and there.
Sage science says to see them there,
    sets them *there* and only there.
And, so, you see, existentially,
    this is just how much *we know*:
Reality's just where we look…
    and, maybe, what *we* conjure up.
Is there perception that, somehow,
    conjoins *us* to reality?
Perceived, it seems, is all that's real,
    while unperceived there is no *me*.

Apotheosis And Betrayal

Consciousness is cancer on the body living.
   Initially offering dynamic vitality—
Enthusiastic growth is very seductive to life—
   consciousness goes on to overwhelm
That body host and fellowship of cells,
   and all that vitality and drive
Turns to incidental destruction
   as mind, transcendent with power
And growth, forsakes that original
   purpose to serve the body whole.
Man's only, extended consciousness
   emerged to serve the body,
But boldly flies free a body's needs,
   and soars with whatever gods,
And aspires beyond biology
   to find and crack the cosmic code.
Evolved to dominate what lives,
   this conscious being
Slips those biological bonds
   that bind it tight to life,
And links its newly freed thoughts
   to other conscious beings,
Distaining that faithful body transport
   that once was master and purpose,
Then dependent and lover....
   And, in the end,
The body's only hope to live
   is that lover's charity.

What?

Life, with all its fluids to live
    and then,
Its dried-out grandeur
    from having lived:
Ah, that the whole, the true story
    be told before it's all over....
From nothing to one cell,
    to dinosaurs, to Man,
To partial, almost understanding,
    to artificial intelligence,
To, then, maybe, answers...
    or not....
And then, at last...
    what?
The poems get shorter,
    perhaps,
Because
    there's nothing more to say.

Biography

Arrogant, yes! and with little justification.
    But there is and was some talent,
A modicum of poetic voice.
    And what he had, wrote and gave,
To anyone who might be interested—
    no strings attached—
Was and is worth a read,
    if only the reader
Will hold their prejudging nose and read
    past the poet and his *biography*.

Out Of The Wilderness

It is often quoted (as advice?) that:
The unexamined life is not worth living.
And the Bible seems to recommend the
wilderness for the site of the examination.
I've been to the wilderness, more than once,
metaphorically—spiritually.
Did I come up, *out of the wilderness*
with a desire to live and do?
No, that's not it…I'm sorry to say.
I'm still here for lack of resolve:
I have found no reason to stay or to go…
so, I just continue to live the mystery.
I think that's the best we can hope for:
to *just continue to live the mystery…*
And go on thinking about everything…
and hope it makes sense to someone…
And participate in life as it unfolds…
and go on refusing to accept fate.…

The Bully

I failed *the bully!*
    I should have kicked his ass.
He was desperately looking
    to find his place in the world
When I chanced upon him.
    But his intimidation was so complete
That I lost my usual self-confidence
    and, succumbing to his threats,
I ran away
    and have forever looked back
Seeing *the bully* as a human monster
    that I should have slayed
To save the world of the meek
    from mere strength,
From fear and loathing,
    from self-hate born of fear.
My epiphany is
    that I owed the world
And *the bully*
    and myself
An ass kicking....
    And,
I can never forgive myself
    for failing us all.

The Shadows Of My Mind

Writing poetry is, for me, a mystery,
　　my truth jumping out of me
From *the shadows of my mind,*
　　from where everything is mine.
It's scary, how insular I am,
　　my thinking, fascinating, *to me,*
With you and you and you just props
　　in my singular stage-show,
Performing for an audience of one,
　　while the world watches in wonder,
Wondering who might be the play-write,
　　and from where-ever has he sprung.
No to all of you.
　　None of you may join my play.
I strut the boards, alone,
　　with a mirror in my hand,
The better to know the artist
　　who paints this world of *me.*
Don't look away, the canvass is huge, and
　　existentialism is what there is to see.

A Little Faster

I finally found myself
    waiting beside the future,
Waiting for the real me
    to come along
And join the life I'd never lived
    while I looked and looked….
Now is always the answer,
    it turns out;
You/I just have to open our eyes
    and run *a little faster.*

To Be The Mother

Before we condemn abortion out of hand,
    perhaps we should consider its purpose:
What if abortion is a form of salvation,
    a pardon from the punishment of being born?
Perhaps earth is, in fact, a vast penal colony
    dedicated to giving aberrant souls
A second chance to live a righteous life
    among their fellow fallen souls,
All those living on earth being inmates
    who are paying for some cardinal sin.
And perhaps the aborting mother
    is the more compassionate person
In this contest between the self-righteous,
    who are intervening in an act of mercy,
And those who rightly perceive our real purpose
    in being alive on earth as being punishment.
Judgement is easy…and sometimes, flawed,
    not always being fairly warranted.
In order to be completely perspicacious,
    we probable need *to* be *the mother.*

Withered

Corruption is to the eager heart
    just as love gone wrong.
Once felt, inevitably grows apace,
    more every lasting breath,
Till all the purity is gone
    and beauty
Becomes sterile to the eye.
    Oh, the heart survives...
Sometimes, forever...
But the bleeding leaves
    it done with love...
And what is left of life
    is forever *withered*.

And I Could Still Sing

I always wanted to sing!
    As a boy, I sang for them,
But I always wanted to sing for me.
    Now time is gone,
Not much left…
    and I have yet/still to sing,
To tell the world, that I missed
    out on,
How much I wanted to sing to it—
    still do….
Running out of time, here,
    and the song is in my throat.
Join me, just this once, World,
    and sing with me,
Sing with me, now, as though
    it were yesterday
And I could sing…
    and I could still sing.

Obnoxiously Capable

Here, attempting to figure out
    what works in life:
I can't help questioning the obvious
    surfeit of intimidating boss-people,
Obnoxiously capable leaders
    who seem to manage the world,
One put-down underling at a time,
    the while treading the toes
Of their peers and superiors
    with equal distain.
Why are there so many/few
    who control our whole lives?
If we didn't need their productivity,
    we'd quit or fire their surly selves.

Man, And His God

I believe that Man created God
    in his own image,
That they, neither, be alone in
    their journey through eternity.

A Child

Fear not my heart,
    I will find you in the dark...
Not in this darkened life
    that keeps us apart,
But in that celestial night
    where our world will be set right.
There is nothing in life
    that can equal love...
So, let's meet and join
    where there's nothing above.
Cause of the wasting heart
    is life that keeps us apart,
But the quest for oneness
    can cause new life to start:
A child, our immortality, genetic
    memory from each our part.

Man

All gone, forever,,,
    all dead…
The best and the brightest,
    the cream of us.
War after war,
    death after death,
Man killing *man,*
    men killing men,
Our destiny.
    What?
Who can go on
    with optimism for us?
How can we—
    this end
As we enter
    and bar behind us
The gates of hell…
    opened by us?
War!
    eternal, endless war
Against us,
    by us.
And we are
    to serve the universe?
Man, the creator?
    Man, the end product?
Man,
    the only living hope….

A Few Seconds

When you need a cigarette,
     a match can be the most
Important thing in the world…
     for *a few seconds*.
That's how life is:
     a few seconds at a time.
And, now, looking back at years,
     all you can see
Are *a few seconds*
     here and there….

Now

Give me one more moment
    and, then,
I will let slip eternity
    from my mind.
Time is always and only:
    Now.
Yesterday and tomorrow
    are illusions.
Be *now.*
    Be only *now.*

No credit!

Toilets should be cleaned.
    Somebody needs to clean them.
It might just as well be me.
    I mean, what else am I
Really good for/can I do
    to contribute to…?
The only really important
    thing that we can do
Is to reproduce,
    keep humanity alive,
Just in case it turns out to be
    a good thing….
I did, but not on purpose—
    only for the pleasure.
No credit for that.
    Maybe, a d-merit.
It was for the wrong reason!
    No credit!
So, do I get to clean the toilets
    or what?

Loneliness

Mitigation was failing to heal the wounds
    and that's when she offered sex.
No tomorrow had not been an option
    until now…
And, suddenly, she was in love.
    Not that romantic chimera
That causes so many tears,
    but the longing to hold onto
What was hers
    and, now, was almost lost.
Reaching out was the last straw.
    The next thing was *loneliness*.

The Road Is Open

She said *no* once too often
    and all the possibilities
Of the road opened, *again*.
    Relationships are all dead-ends.
Tomorrow is only possible
    if you believe it's there.
So, how much, and when?
    The road is open.

Firefly?

Nowhere I saw one flash
    in the dark…and no more.
Was that another life
    winking hello, goodbye,
A fellow mind,
    calling out in the dark,
Or,
    was it just one lost *firefly*?

Happy Place

Christopher Kerr, a career, hospice doctor,
    has been researching patient's dreams
For over forty years.
    Dr. Kerr is convinced of,
And has written a book detailing,
    end of life, comfort dreams,
Dreams which would seem to connect
    his patients with dead comforters.
He documents particularly vivid dreams
    which connect the patients to
Already dead people
    (and sometimes animals)
Who are waiting for the dying
    to join them in a *happy place.*
Oneiromancy has never been
    so scientific or mainstream.

Standoffish

Childhood torment, that he forgot—
    someone said: *must be repressed*—
Clear symptoms, but no memories,
    a blessing's what consensus guessed.
Most likely true, I hate to touch,
    and never kiss unless I must.
No one's allowed to know my heart,
    not you *or I*—can't seem to trust.
Alone at tables made for two
    at Burger King or Hardies,
Alone in stores, at checkout stands,
    alone at crowded parties.
You'll seldom find me in a crowd,
    but, if occasion means I must,
I'm somewhere in the very back,
    alone and visible, but just.
I used to pass him in the store.
    Now his name is etched in stone.
He told his name, but nothing more,
    in what I'd call a civil tone.
Not local, talked some Yankee talk,
    from way up north— maybe D.C.,
Or somewhere from the Middle West,
    no place for southerners to be.
He needed help, but wouldn't ask.
    Standoffish: Wore it like a mask.

Whatever's Left Of You

As the mind slips away,
    all that you've learned
Leaves you in inverse progression,
    imperceptible at first,
Then more and more
    there's less and less
Of the you that you've become
    till all that's left
Is what you brought when born:
    primal you in a dying hearse,
And all your thoughts are of
    genetic immortality:
The next forever generation,
    the survival of life, and, then,
Acceptance that your part in this
    tragedy is over, and that you
Have only to give away and leave
    whatever's left of you.

A Different Bloom

This one's blooming was seen
    as manifestation of giving—
All about her grew in stature
    through reaping what she sowed.
Her intellect reflected an inner beauty
    mirroring the best of her peers.
She, a paragon of perfection,
    drew from each his best.
While, an island of serenity,
    she coolly went her sparkling way,
And where her talent dazzled,
    lesser writers fell into line.
As for beauty, all know it
    when they read her work.

Threatening The Moon

Speak neither person.
    Send little ripples of truth
Across the chasm of consciousness
    stimulating anything that's waiting.
Cross that border for words
    and feelings,
Step up to life *for me*,
    take what you need,
Then run back into the enchantment of you,
    laughing at the trick you've played.
Ignore the smirks and mirrors:
    You're the last one *threatening the moon*.

The Six Pillars Of Love
(Love Defined And Idealized)

Shared mutual needs
    and desires.
Enlightened, mutual,
    self-interest and goals.
Committed, empathetic,
    mutual support.
Relationship, intentionally,
    put above self-interest.
The self, intentionally, sacrificed
    to the relationship.
Intention of eternal,
    total integration.

A Heart To Hold Onto

That promised goodnight
    has slowly turned to empty darkness…
Still, I see myself not judge but judged
    as truth invades my soul.
Stand, open heart, I need you now:
    I need your longings
And your innocence…
    and, yes, the romance of you
As I begin to turn away
    from faithless life
And start my long goodbye,
    close out the artifice of light
And fasten on the certainty
    of never interrupted sleep.
Those promises were not to be
    but were for me
Deceptions revealed
    in purgatory's light,
So, I have ceased
    expecting their rewards.
But trust and use of truth—
    redemption by your love—
Can alter future beacons
    for one driven to the dark.
And I, who see this forfeit future,
    need *a heart to hold onto.*

Always Yours
or
What You Can Have

I am more than apparition—Less than real—
    just quick enough of wit and word to tickle
Your self-image with the fantasy that spurs
    regeneration and human progress alike.
Don't try to touch my hand—I'm not a tactual,
    sensual reward, but am a promise to be savored
In a moment here and there—something you could have,
    but shouldn't have— but are encouraged to want…
A stimulating thought—an exciting idea to fill
    idle moments with hopes and dreams of pleasures
That are never really felt or seen…but are no less real….
    Have me whenever you want—whenever you can….
Dream me, love me—enjoy the hell out of me,
    I'm always there, in your heart for the taking:
So, take every possible hope and pleasure into your own
    hands, in my name, and while remembering me!
And I'm real for words, for talk, for feedback:
    so real that you can more than imagine me.
But, like an ephemeral reflection in calm water,
    it takes but a single touch to lose me, forever….

Abortion?

Only for immortals is life worth living:
　　Immortals with total recall;
Sentient, thinking beings
　　for whom there is no time
Only experiences to fill the void
　　where time would be.
For mortals—with little past
　　and less future—
Now must give and fill and feel and be
　　everything at once...
And that's just too much to ask or find,
　　to wait for or to miss....
Abortion should not only be legal, but
　　praised, encouraged, sought and done.
If there is real compassion for children,
　　don't have them/force them to live.
Nihility is individually inevitable.
　　　Why not accept and act on that truth?

Orphaned Poems

Poems that are different are often homeless.
    Readers are hesitant to invite them
Into their minds, into their thinking.
    Different prospectives cause discomfort.
Poetry people, although a tolerant bunch,
    tend to be quite conventional
When it comes to things like subject matter
    that draws and repels at the same time.
Even though their own thoughts occasionally
    (too often?) may stray into such thoughts,
They are hesitant to invest uncertainty
    in an unknown, unvetted source.
Well, I contend that every subject, even if
    repellant, deserves a reading—consideration—
A thought or two before being shutout—tossed—
    as thoughts, maybe, getting too close to home….
Poems by unknowns—strangers—should
    be judged on impact…and dismissed
Only when the reader *doesn't* have an *I never*
    thought about it that way, moment…or two.

Still Standing

Come lightning, aim your lash at me,
    display your deadly symmetry;
Let your searing fire flow
    into my troubled soul below;
Strike what you will that's left of me.
    Your threat of death is always bound
By those already gone to ground
    and buried in the heart of me
And stolen—lost—where I can't see,
    to leave me primed but out of time,
To stand, erect, defiant, strong…
    to face your threat and all that's wrong.
Take what you will, there is no doubt:
    The best are gone and I'm left out.
Go tell your master, Death, for me:
    I stand to speak…*and then to shout!*

Life, Love, Legacy And Me

Here I am,
    older than I thought I'd be.
No fair complaints,
    except that nagging question, *Why?*
And believing in the hoped for three
    of *life and love and legacy.*
Life because without which, naught,
    and with no love there's just ennui,
And, last, there's legacy:
    That's what we leave of life,
And love: Our plan and foundation
    for a better world.
While life and love are for us now,
    legacy's for generations yet to come,
What we leave for them, *or is that, too,*
    for us…? in fact, our genes are *they.*
Our duty is our sacrifice for them:
    our reaching, grasping for immortality.
That's existential…so, you see,
    we always come right back to *me.*

The Poet's Gift

You see, the poet is a poem himself,
    a series of cosmic truths
Unwinding in time,
    suspended in space, in time,
And held in place by words in kind,
    dangled as bait
Just so to cause,
    then catch a thought—or two;
He is a catalyst—a spark—perhaps:
    the spark, the only spark,
To light our way
    through time and space—
Yesterday
    and then tomorrow…
To catch and hold
    reality by the tail
And to make mankind *the* thing
    to be reckoned with:
A light in eternal darkness:
    Meaning where there's none:
A force in the universe:
    Its measure
And the thought
    that prods time on its way.
The poet's words,
    after all,
Are all that we really are…
    creation is then *his* creation
And the gods or God,
    his gifts.

Evolution's Stepchildren

If we are to be true to life—
    the preciousness of its gift:
That it evolves on God's advice,
    that life is its own prize,
Not diamonds, gold or blue skies,
    or the theory of relativity
And all that math might mean or be—
    not even inertia and gravity,
Then the requirement is truth and honesty:
    We must cherish mosquitoes and lice,
Bacteria, viruses, plague and HIV
    (all of which live to evolve new life).
Or, maybe not. Maybe mistakes were made.
    Maybe failure is the cost of success…
Or, maybe, perfection is the price that's paid!
    Or maybe failure *is* final success…
Maybe God is another mistake *we* made.
    And, *maybe,* we can't be saved!

To Be Or Not To Be

I would flee into that darkness
    where there is nothing to find or lose,
Nothing to come back from
    while fearing that there's nothing to fear,
Where there is no reason to stay or leave—
    to be or not to be—
No reason to serve the flesh or heart,
    to serve love or hate or reason.
I will go where most of my friends have gone,
    where *their* time stopped,
Where *their* suffering ended,
    where *they* embraced that last refuge.
I will flee into the calm of nothing
    and rest with those at rest.

Orphaned Poems II

Awaken from my spell—and never mind
    this ending of my story,
    this parting with my time....
But if you must seek out
    the valley precincts of my mind:
    read, carefully,
    these *orphaned poems* I've left behind:
Their mirror images
    will pierce your view,
    whose memories will define my life,
    and all those images will be from you.
Don't expect my words
    to set *you* free,
    these poems were crafted
    to comfort *me*;
Most themes emerged
    from eerie, mystic dreams
    full of pure ideals,
    not flesh and blood it seems;
And there are no secrets,
    none that aren't here shorn:
    whom you find here was not
    and never will be born.

What Does He See?

One night I woke
    to a living dream
Of a little boy,
    face all agleam;
His future self
    is me it seems.
At play I see
    his smiling face
As phantom friends
    join in his chase;
Oh, how I long
    to take his place.
With stick for sword
    and vision grand,
Each toy responds
    to his command
And leads to triumph
    in the sand.
Then, suddenly,
    fate cast the dice,
His gaze turned on me
    like a vise,
His stare seemed fixed
    upon our life.
That cheerful smile
    soon fades away;
The fun seems gone,
    he stops his play;
His thoughts enmesh
    with mine today.

And if that boy
    can really see
What I've become,
    what he will be:
Does that mean he
    Is ashamed of me?

How Close We Came

All these fond words
    disturb like rain:
They speed my heart
    while dulling pain.
Reading, hearing,
    remembering, too,
Whichever I choose,
    it conjures you:
You, whom I know,
    but who will not see,
You whose heart
    has no room for me.
So, cheering myself,
    I call up fond words,
Expressions of love
    that you never heard.
Do not turn away.
    Do not pity me.
I am what I am
    and will always be.
And, when you hear
    the patter of rain,
Remember, *please*,
    how close we came.
Then you might smile
    at that thought of me,
Like a summer's shade
    that's caress is free.

Women

Girls, ladies, *women* are sacred:
    They are victims of life:
They literally bleed for life.
    And they are driven to procreate,
Without which, nothing:
    no Man, no humanity, no civilization,
No challenging of the gods:
    neither Olympics nor Olympics.
Men are all the sons of *women*,
    and mankind itself their creation.
God is for another time, another poem:
    Men's excuse for denying the truth.

Dream

I always knew that dreams
    were dreams
With pleasures that,
    on waking up,
Were left as dreams
    and only dreams….
You were a *dream,*
    still are a *dream,*
Will always be
    my favorite *dream…*
And best for me,
    I won't wake up
From dreaming you,
    my nightly *dream,*
And wide awake
    and living *dream.*

Beyond A Lover's Chain

Exsanguination from my heart,
    displaying what the heart contains,
Splashing past my other thoughts
    like flooding when it rains.
And you, so close—right there you were—
    my thoughts were lost to speech.
So close, within my easy grasp,
    yet wholly out of reach.
I waited for some hint of hope
    to break inertia's chain,
Or anything to staunch the breach
    that widened with my pain,
While you would gaily chatter past,
    as though I were not there—
There, where I can't help but be,
    but where you didn't deign to care....
So far, the travails of my heart
    have stiffened my resolve
And, playing even this small part,
    gives hope room to evolve.
If waiting for your love to start
    is all that's left for me,
Then, seeking what will never be,
    is mine to cheer eternity.

Please Don't Be Me

When you are what you shouldn't be,
    you still can act out differently—
Compensate—pretend a lot,
    but still you'll always just be you…
Until you die still being you.
    You know the world must often change,
Yet you won't change—you just cannot—
    so let it go, the world I mean,
And die on time, or even soon,
    but first address man's mound of sin
And teach your kids to live and be
    the persons that you should have been.

Do It All Again

Her first memories were of her father,
  of competing with the world
For his attention, for the love
  that she never became sure of.
School, and all the boys would look,
  laugh, be mean, then run away…
Till, one day, she and they stopped looking
  and began reaching and touching….
She had a daughter, and tried to explain
  to the child why not to touch that way.
She had a granddaughter, and tried again
  to teach her how to keep the boys away.
She told three generations of mothers
  to ignore the demands of their bodies—
Why none of them should have been,
  but, in her heart, *she'd do it all again.*

Live In Your Moment

All the young heroes will fight and die
    and die and die and die and die:
Which was *his* cause? Does it still matter
    once time has run and loosed him to fly?
Which war will kill us,
    which will it be?
Heroes, we hope, decide progeny:
    genetic lines, who will we be?
Who will we dominate,
    what will they do?
Which species wins?
    Who knows? Are they new?
Will they last? Is it true?
    Do you know? Was it you?
Does it matter?
    Does it matter?
Evolution keeps speaking
    through fossils and genes
Of endless editions,
    of lost lines, it seems:
Gone after triumph
    and never returned,
What lessons are told?
    What lessons are earned…?

Seize all the castles,
    the women, the gold,
The days you can live,
    but know you can't hold?
Instead we should learn,
    learn all that we can,
And grasp all the truth
    no matter how grim,
And laugh at that truth…
    and live our grim whim.

Change: One Certainty

One certainty:
    Time is sure to kill me…
If I have the patience
    to wait for change.
What a revelation: a lifetime
    of work—of change—
And I've mastered
    my world—
Then I find that all
    I ever had to do was live.
And, if I hadn't changed,
    I'd be immortal,
And if immortal,
    I wouldn't change.
Certainty, it seems,
    is an uncertain comfort
And one that ends
    in silence.
Death is forever:
    immortal—without change.
Nature, *the there that's there,*
    is certain—changeable.
Choose any prayer
    with care.

Outré

Outré is how the world treats those
    who ask for explanation of outrage,
And expiation for excess—
    that being, then, what seems to us
And them and everyone, correct,
    and yes, and yes and yes, called for.
Outre's the odd, right-sounding word
    for wreaking cultural homicide—
The live world's way of answering
    dumb questions asked about itself.
The French, only, can sneer and say
    outré the prickly, proper way
To leave the dunders trapped, belittled,
    peevish and inclined to fight.
Never fail to appreciate
    the power of sincere insult.
The outraged world speaks *outré* French
    with more distain than is France's fault.

A Line Of Beauty

A line of beauty
    inside my head
Flourishing there without
    a hope it will be said.
These words
    I dedicate to you
Who know, also,
    they can't come true.
Hope's distance
    is not too far to say,
To close my eyes
    and let you come my way.
Why write these words
    but never say to you?
You must not hear—
    it's best you never knew.
Look back, just once,
    then quickly go your way;
We dare not start,
    you knew I would not stray.
Remember nothing,
    except my desperate stare...
There is no future
    waiting for you here.

Barred From Paradise

He was empathy incarnate,
 a haunted psyche
Smoldering against the indignities
 of cannibalism,
The curse
 of all things mortal,
With tasty exception
 of those single celled
Mortals
 adept at digesting
Organic chemicals
 into proteins that become and are
The foundation
 of our deadly food pyramid.
Prosperity is a belly filled
 with someone else's protean.
And our morality
 consigns us all to hell
For feeding appetites
 that are *barred from paradise.*

Our Kindest Words Are Lies

Our kindest words are lies:
To the terminal child: *The shot*
    will make you sleep for a little while,
    then, when you wake, it'll be
    Christmas Day, presents you've dreamed of,
    the best dinner, ever—
    everything you ever wanted.
    My tears? I'm so happy for you.
    Now one more kiss, until tomorrow…
    I mean, the whole family will be there,
    together, for the best day ever.
Love*: You're more attractive than ever, my dear.*
    These decades have brought out
    the best in your aspect and temperament.
    Not to worry about me.
    I never even think of anyone else.
    Why radishes when I've a peach at home?
Competition: You were great,
    The toughest competitor(s) ever.
Prosaic: *So you lost your:*
    Job, boy/girlfriend, scholarship, money.
    There's more of everything out there, waiting.
    Now let's see that smile.

For the poet: *You're too good to be understood, means:*
    Pearl before swine. Forget it. Let's dine.
Warfare: *You're sure to lose and die.*
    Surrender and we'll treat you like equals.
    You have nothing to fear from us.
    We're just here to make you free.
Hospice: *Of course there's God—afterlife.*
    You're on a cosmic quest.
    The future just gets better and better.
The kindest words, and, sometimes,
    the noblest, *are lies.*

Yours Or Mine?

There is no time left.
    Give me what you have to give.
We must share all, *now*.

No Secrets Anymore

How many secrets does a man
    have to take to the grave
To make himself heard?
    How much do you know
That no amount of saying or writing
    or good will can give away?
Who doesn't reach out, every day,
    to other people only to be rebuffed
By the sheer impossibility
    of real commingling of thought?

Reach as far as you will—
    as far as you can:
All you'll ever feel is your own fingertips
    pressing against the outsides
Of things that you can't get inside of.
    Don't fool yourself again:
You're what you are, and all you've got,
    and the only one who is listening.
Every man's a hero in his own head.
    And there are *no secrets anymore.*

What Is Real

Come with me now on a word quest,
    to a place where words prevail.
Though corporeal me dissolve,
    gone soon, as such things always go,
These words, my words, will be to you
    more me than I could ever be.
Now hear the whispers in your mind,
    hear my thoughts, not what I said:
That there was never any we,
    but only me inside my head
Looking out at lonely worlds—
    at universes not yet dead.
Knowing looking's mere illusion
    with its mirrored, hearing, feeling.
Knowing's real but not the known.
    Known exists, but all alone.

True Words

True for a moment—
 more than that, we seldom say.
I love you. Pass the salt.
 Do you think it will rain today?
When I said those words,
 they completely filled my mind:
Thoughts all-important, at the time.
 Now, looking back, I find
Some served the purpose
 of making known my needs;
Some sounded boastful,
 bragging on my deeds;
Some were conversation:
 There's always purpose in that;
Some were expletives:
 Words we use to spat;
But words I spoke
 of me and you
Were from my heart,
 and every word's still true.

Thoughts Of Me

Anything is better than nothing
    is rather noticed than ignored.
Love is too rare to find:
    Any passion must do.
Hate is a primary passion,
    rising as pure emotion,
More lasting than love,
    more tenacious than mirth,
Focusing attention on itself
    while crowding out all else.
What a gift to be the lasting focus
    of my enduring fantasy:
Here's hoping that *you* forever seethe
    at the slightest *thought of me.*

Or Maybe Hope

He never understood
    his own drinking…
Though he had tried
    from time to time.
It never made any sense,
    that fatalistic desire
To end today—
    by force—
And take his chances
    with tomorrow.

Celebration

Fresh grave, new to the passing eye,
    with unbowed flowers, pageant-like,
Signs of a *celebration* joined—
    or one to come—with singing saved
For Sundays sounding in the silence
    as honored guest is closed from light.
Tears, perhaps, like mine now welling,
    though I know none buried here.
How much more we fancy parting
    than our screaming, outraged birth:
Squirming pilgrims in distress
    evicted from our mother's womb,
Newborns cry for help and mercy
    nescient of their certain doom.

Let Me Go There

There is my place, yesterday.
 I go *there* often.
No one *there* is *here*,
 but I live *here* and *there*.
Some new friends are *here*,
 but the old, the best are *there*.
My choice is always *there*,
 but *here* holds body fast,
And body draws mind *here*.
 Urge, loss and pain, all *here*.
But *there* holds heart—
 heart's hopes lie *there*.
New friends, conscience—
 tethering life—
Let me go!
 Let me go there.

What I Think

If life is more than dust,
    what then in life is just?
Why then my life?
    Why yours?
Why were we born,
    if not to breech forbidden doors—
If not to create places,
    where,
We live our lives
    more blissfully—
I know this how?
    I know internally!
I know it when
    your smile is free
And when I hear your voice,
    lilting on the phone,
As though
    welcoming me home;
I know it when
    you laugh at me
And when you ignore
    my stupidity;

I know it when
    you touch my arm that way,
As though to say:
    What you want, you may.
I know it when my thoughts
    are full of you each day;
I know it as you hold
    my every dream in sway.
These words are written
    just for you,
If you believe them,
    be committed, too,
Say my words are not a whim—
    say these thoughts are true.

Complete The Cycle

This poem is for my children, two:
     I pray I'm in your memory.
And grandchildren, for all of you,
     this poem is I when I'm not me.
You eight are my imprint on life,
     the legacy of our forebears.
Our genes are passed from me through you,
     the promise kept for each who cares.
Of all the hopes man thinks to have—
     love, honor, truth and, oh yes, fate—
Love only will transcend our deaths,
     your lives are proof we had that trait.
That we exist is all the proof
     there is that we should pass our genes.
Eternal duty so far done,
     the spark keeps kindled mankind's dreams.
Each generation must decide
     if culture and our art extends—
If future will be worth the pain,
     or whether procreation ends.

But education is the curse
    that may soon prove we stand on sand.
Pursue the truth that's *yours* to find,
    then *you* decide the fate of Man.
Shakespeare was right: cowards live on…
    bare bodkins seldom are their fate.
Less honor, hands to murder turn,
    then trust decisions jurors make.
All you can hope for is today.
    Tonight, you'll close your eyes and beam
Beyond those things you thought you may
    into, perhaps, another dream.
Tomorrow finds you where you lay,
    no longer who or what you seem.
So be yourself for just this day—
    be who you are and what you say.
Complete the cycle, live then die.
    And, seeking truth? *You have to try.*

Cogitators

The depth and cogence of a mind
  is best measured
By the number of diametric views
  simultaneously held.
What I have thought,
  then crafted into poems,
Although inconsistent,
  even to my sympathetic eye,
Is all the immortality
  that's available to *me.*
Enough, then. Not satisfied,
  but finished—through.
Read and think my words anew...
  then sublimate what's me.
I stand in the deep valley of my mind,
  one foot in the void of grave,
One foot on the ascent of Olympus,
  full of fear and chutzpah.
If what I've written of my thought
  adds half the shadow of one neutrino
To what the reader is to become,
  I've done what few have done.
Not satisfactory, of course,
  but worthy of *cogitators.*
And don't get me started on the
  futility of poetry.
Against the cosmic winds beat
  the phenomena of arrogant life.

To Try To Please

These words forever
    tempt my tongue:
I tried to please,
    but pleased no one.

My Fantasizing Man

I'm not the man *he* wants to be,
    but still he often comes to me
And brings a special synergy,
    my fantasizing man.
The things he does are sometimes bad,
    more often though, they make me glad,
But then, again, sometimes sad,
    my fantasizing man.
Who waking ever has more fun
    than he who never has to run
From beast or man or even gun:
    My fantasizing man.
And when it comes to great romance,
    he's always first to start the dance—
He never hesitates to prance—
    my fantasizing man.
The love from all he's there to take,
    he makes not even one mistake,
No lover can his love forsake,
    my fantasizing man.

And, if the gods indeed abide,
    and from them nothing can I hide,
I fear his antics they will chide,
    my fantasizing man.
But life may really be a dream,
    and things are never what they seem,
More to the point, I can't redeem
    my fantasizing man.
And when at last my dreams stand still,
    and I am buried in the hill,
He'll never feel the slightest chill,
    my fantasizing man.

At Half To 666

Let me dream that I'm a dreamer,
    of what may be and might have been.
Let me hope that I am hopeful,
    and hope remains a part of men.
When life despairs and I don't care
    what happens in that life,
Let me seek another choice—
    some good to come of strife.
And when I wake and find the world
    all smiling, fresh and new,
Let's join hands to wrought and hold
    a better place for me and you.
I woke one night to find the clock
    was stuck at 333.
The devil's path was clear to see
    at half way down to 666,
Implicitly it threatened me
    from the other side of Styx.
It's not how many days are lost
    that can't return to me,
It's that I have to pay the cost
    to let my soul fly free.
Tomorrow I may fail, again,
    perhaps to drown in willful sin;
Today, however, just might be
    when hope and life begin.

Afterthought

Nature does things
    and men do things.
Now men have begun
    their sprint.
Nature had its way with things,
    to make and break,
    to build and mold,
    for millennia—from forever ago.
All done, nature did
    —everything—
    until yesterday:
    the sky, the rocks, the land…
    then an *afterthought*,
    an aberration:
    Nature then made man.
Eternity to do so much,
    in seconds men unwound her secrets,
    one after one.
Then, reaching out for all at once,
    for the apple and the stars,
    Intuitively we unlock the cosmic DNA,
    a cancerous grasp of a few genes
    here and there,
Then ecstasy of perceptive insight,
    then transcendent discovery,
Then an orgy of destruction…
    then, perhaps, *just perhaps,*
    regurgitated *afterthought.*

Our Last Cavalier

A crazy old man,
>   who went to war to die,
To save a world,
>   or, at least, to try...
But the war
>   had passed him by—
Bereft
>   of gore and glory.
Drilling every day,
>   to pay the battle's cost
(Already fought...
>   those memories long lost).
Making muster
>   in empty ranks,
To shield civilians
>   who show no thanks,
And facing enemies
>   too much like him to fear,
Lost from the care
>   of those who will not hear,
Who only stop
>   to look and jeer....
As dead as good
>   the world has said,

And better that
    than listen to his ravings.
He cannot fight
    the dreaded dead—
There is no blood
    for him to shed—
No comrades marching
    to his stead…
So, alone,
    he lives in dread:
    our last Cavalier.

Where I Stay

Tears flow too often from the eye,
    for love, for greatness, for goodbye.
Rain soaks the cleverest shelter through,
    then waters life, then washes out.
What's common's wet and honest truth:
    genetic memory retold.
Wait for the dawn and light, and life—
    if there's a smile, it's surely there.
Awake, again? Tomorrow waits,
    and all that's lost awaits you then.
Who stays who doesn't long to go?
    Who goes who doesn't long to wait?
The pain is when more wait than wake,
    and sleep, impatient, is too slow:
When memories were waiting here
    and then are gathered for you there.
To sleep is not to leave—to go—
    but coming home to all you know.
Disturbing dreams, and then I wake,
    uncertain where I'd rather be.
The dream, when dreamt becomes the real,
    and days, awaiting dreams, too long.
No more are mornings time to rise,
    Now rising's calling from night skies.
Awake, asleep, seem both the same—
    my ghosts await with like disdain.
No need to hurry either way.
    I'm home no matter *where I stay.*

Oh God

My greatest fear in life,
    in an existential reality,
Is that I awaken to find
    that *I* am God,
And, that all that is,
    I have created;
That I have the power
    to manipulate reality,
To make whatever I will
    out of raw reality,
Out of a string theory
    or out of nothing…
That I am that I am,
    that I know everything,
That I am everywhere that is,
    that I am one of a kind…
And, but for the toys I've made,
    I am alone in this my lonely universe.

To Go Back Home

The first cup of the day is gone and, again,
    I awoke in yesterday's tomorrow.
Mornings are always about tomorrow,
    but all we know is yesterday.
Life's like that,
    full of hope…and nostalgia.
Why does time only become tomorrow
    when we could accomplish so much more
Yesterday?
    Yesterday we know just what to do,
But tomorrow is a mystery
    waiting in ambush for life.
Did you ever notice that we all
    want to wake up tomorrow…
But that we all
    want *to go back home* to die?

No More To Beam

Count down to nothing,
    and I'm leaving soon.
Goodbye is such a common,
    over used word,
That it has long since lost finality.
    But finality is the destination
When death intercedes,
    like the benevolent friend that it is,
And takes charge:
    When life willingly submits,
Flickering weakly
    in gesture of resignation
And then is gone,
    no more to beam *tomorrow…*
No more to beam…
    no more to be….

Don't Wait For Me

Think on my face,
　　my words, my place…
Where your memory rises to meet me,
　　I'm still there.
When you come to find just where
　　you looked away and lost me,
I'm waiting there.
　　It's all about *you*, you know?

And what of me?
　　Without notice, or tears,
I just slipped away,
　　ever so quietly,
Into that mist of half-truths
　　and myth and faded memory:
Was I real…or just some cartoon
　　character you thought you knew?
And I won't be back…
　　not even for your promises….

Might-Have-Been

Did you love me, once,
  long time ago,
When I deliberately
  did not love you?
Are you remembering me,
  when I don't remember you?
If only hopes could realize,
  your dream might now be true....
But time is closed and gone.
  Time does not wait but waste....
Time now to cherish
  might-have-been,
Time to taste your dream again...
  as some delicious sin.

Time's Getting Shorter

3 a. m. and sleep has ended in failure.
    There was no rest, only furious dreaming.
Never know.
    It comes and goes: Sleep.
Sleep used to be a way to sort things out,
    dream up answers,
But *time's getting short…*
    answers never seem to last.
What I knew isn't true anymore…
    dementia, maybe.
Lots of guys are doing that.
    Next is pretty much a question mark.
Should I try to sleep again? Dream?
    Wrestle those same questions?
Or get out of bed
    and do things,
Find something worth wanting,
    think about what I wish I'd done,

Or do stuff I'm tired of doing?
    I used to like to drink and eat,
To touch other people—
    you know, sex—
To talk and go, get out and drive...
    but no more.
Now I sit and TV and read
    and think about thinking.
A lot of questions...
    no one listens.
They talk,
    but they don't hear.
I've got money,
    but not answers...no truth.
And I'm tired,
    really tired.
I guess it's about time...
    I think it's time.

Extreme Unction

Extreme unction:
    Words I do not dread,
Time means nothing,
    when you're already dead.
It's a mind-set thing:
    Priest robed in black,
The color of death,
    both mean the same
To mortals, marooned,
    who wish they never came.
Time means nothing
    back to when you died,
Life had ended
    and you knew exactly why:
A sickened heart
    for what you didn't try...
Extreme unction,
    and, at last, goodbye.

Anonymous Me

The deal I made with life,
   anonymous me, is this:
To take without getting
   and give without taking—
To stay out of sight
   in either case;
To be me, *all of the time,*
   no matter how badly I want to be you;
To chase phantoms in my head,
   while the rest of you chase life;
To accept that I'm lost,
   while you all find each other;
To know that I know that I don't know,
   while everybody else seems to know;
To hide while society hands out souls,
   then cry for a soul;
To be invisible in front of the crowd,
   while I lead the crowd in search of…
To wake up every hour in the night,
   wishing that I could sleep;
To sleep and sleep and sleep,
   while the rest of you don't;
To believe in what I say,
   while hearing you not hearing me;
To write this poem tonight
   and to tear it up tomorrow.

Word Weaving

Snatch the commonest of words,
    fresh from anonymous mouths,
And temper them with intellect
    till all their meaning speaks,
Then claim them to be yours,
    to offer up as gifts,
Then declare them boldly
    upon the sonic air,
Then filter all their syllables—
    each word, each sentence—
Through your computer
    to set them clearly down
In neat and reverent rows
    upon the blank, impatient page,
Just so to quench the genius
    of thoughts beyond the brain
And leave the readers wondering
    what the hell was meant.

Alone

I am one biological cell
    in the infinite mind of God,
One tiny grain of sand
    on an endless beach,
One star burning in open space,
    in a night bright with stars,
All of which have risen
    to shine for just one night,
To test the dark—*to guide to light?*
    to send photons to find forever...
How could any cell, any grain of sand,
    any star, complain of *loneliness?*

No More...No Less....

Good men, not needing or asking for more
     or enough of the world's bounty,
Who have never stopped seeking reasons
     to disbelieve,
Who have passed on science,
     to find personal salvation in faith
And God in the privation of cell and self:
     Holy Men, who have spoken to the devil,
Challenging him to win their souls—
     living in silent vows and lingering doubt,
Searching the only thing they know—
     the crevices of their lonely thoughts—
For one more piece of knowledge
     they may have overlooked,
That, taken by surprise, may quiet the fear
     that never lets their longings rest—
While genetic need tugs
     at the edge of being,
Promising immortality
     through the delights of procreation:
These saints' rewards are exactly
     what they are willing to accept,
No more...
     no less....

Another Dead End

Nature has done,
    so do, too, Men.
But time itself is nature,
    no act in hast—
Lest some mistake—
    no imperfection left
To mar the symmetry
    in reality.
But Man's
    grasshopper actions
Light here and there
    in reality—
Coincident after
    coincidental act—
With all results
    a mystery.
Too many of nature's
    secrets learned,
We deflower her perfections…
    she turns on our affront….
And back we go
    to elemental state,
Our threat to stasis
    swept clean for vanity.
And we: *Another dead-end,*
    closed line of evolution.
This much and more to come.
    I tell you, friends,
It's time to listen
    to Gaea's admonitions.

Companionship

Emotions are the goal we seek,
    and, mostly, *hate* and *love*,
To meld with one another's love
    and then, to hate, appears the same.
Our greatest gift's *companionship*,
    the prize we can withhold or give.
Love must then *be* companionship,
    and hate its next of kin.
Companionship is what we seek,
    while death's escape from loneliness.
Emotion leads to quickened life,
    So, quickened life would seem the goal.
And quickened life and then a rest
    is clearly manifest in sex.
The salmon mates, lays eggs and dies—
    those fertile eggs worth all the strife.
Emotions, though, might compromise
    how evolution sustains life.

Fire Or Venom?

Sometimes there's fire,
        sometimes venom
        rising from my breast…
And I still don't know
        which way is best.

Fire seeks a crowd around
        and warms them all,
        and asks them each
        to join him at his dance;
Then, pulling them towards himself,
        he leaves no independent breath
        and cast them all
        upon their startled backs.

Not venom's game at all:
One each, and only
        at the call.
        they come to say goodbye—
        and leaving at once,
        never know just why.

Fidelity

Love comes and goes,
    but never stands defined.
And, when we many hope
    to make our little lives worthwhile,
We call on love—we turn to love:
    Love we had, or almost had,
Or love we never had at all.
    And then we say that love
Is what our lives should consist of—
    is what we need to fill our dreams....
Yet, all the while, we smile
    and go about our simple chores
Of sharing what we have
    with all those souls
Who also struggle, daily,
    with hopes and dreams of love.
And there, in doing for each other,
    in sharing life, fear and hope,
Lost in simple thoughts and acts and words,
    is what we're really most about:
The empathetic charity that binds mankind:
    Fidelity is the true glue of life.

Found And Lost

If you were to read my poems,
    but, instead of words,
    see mirrored thoughts,
Then those poems
    would serve us both
By disproving my greatest fear:
    But there is no one but me.

Identity

His personality
  was such—
And his intellect
  concurred—
That he really
  had to live
  alone.
His relationship
  with mankind
  was so
  circumscribed
That he had to be
  mankind—
  and that alone.
This contradiction
  led him on
  to bizarre plots
  and suicidal rage...
But promises
  to himself
Drew him back,
  and he stayed
  in fold
  from day to day—
Today...
  and hopefully,
  tomorrow.

The Dark Key

Unless you are inside of something, there is
    no place in the whole universe that is dark:
How is it then that we need
    the darkness in order to dream?
And then, when we dream, how is it
    that the dream is always lit?
Is *darkness the key*, the entrance into
    some other universe or dimension
To which we are drawn, from time to time,
    from which to look back, through the dark
And put prospective in our lives,
    in this existence—or perhaps: in the other?
If the answer is yes, then where are we—
    exactly—and what time is it right now?

The Mensch

They hated him for his pride and for
    his cockiness and for his swagger,
And the only time that he was really
    popular was when trouble came.
But when his fighter plane erupted
    into a fireball, and his only chance
To live was to bail out immediately,
    Colonel Santini calmly turned his
Aircraft out to sea and away from
    people on the ground, and then
Radioed the control tower. The last
    words they heard him to say were:
So long, ladies! This is the Great
    Santini doing it right, as usual.

Easter Message, 2006
Greater love hath no man...

Yesterday's News

Yesterday's newspaper, cartwheeling
    down, across the street,
Flailing in the wind,
    carrying away all the old news,
Already read, about the great and dead,
    people's stories, *over now...*
What's happening today
    soon humming in the printing press.
A hapless, stray cat, crossing the street,
    suddenly terrified by
The ghosts of yesterday,
    rushing to haunt everyone's memory.

Facing Down Death

Let's get this show on the road,
    he said, as he pulled off his oxygen mask.
That's how Judge Powell faced life
    and that's how the Judge chose to die.

That Time Of Year

The holiday season has stalked me
    for almost a year now.
As the days of torment approach,
    I walk less through the crowd
And keep a wary tongue:
    The slightest hint of kindness
Invites a grab or grasp—
    everybody wants something.

Down in the woods on the farm,
    my last retreat, I make my stand;
But the mail, and the radio, and TV,
    and worst of all:
The whine of the phone
    pursues and claws at my conscience.

Never mind your pain, they say—
    never mind the haunted corridors
Of the shuttered memories
    where the last of your friends,
And allies and dreams have retreated
    before your desperate pursuit;
Never mind yourself—
    come do for us—
Empty your soul into our desires—
    and shut up about it!

The Drain

Racing on toward the dark,
    to find whatever I have lost,
Pushing aside cadavers, death,
    looking for purity of thought:
Books, or, better, mystic poems
    consumed, voraciously, page by page,
A line or phrase or word I find,
    highlight them all, or underline.
Hurrying on,
    I fall behind.
And where's the light
    I strove to find?
Not here...nowhere...
    It's lost in time.
Turn back—not clock,
    but me—my brain.
Not running on, but draining out...
    It's wasted down *the drain*.

Unlost Souls

Salt is the cartilage—
    soft bones of the sea—
Just so the mystic being
    in soft tissue brain.
And, as the sun mists salt
    from out the body of the sea,
The heat of living life dries
    the soul from out the brain
And leaving salt dry,
    and alone, and still wanted,
The sea impatiently laps
    at the margin sands of land—
Incessantly demanding back
    that skeleton it lost—
Its legacy redeeming
    where it can.
So life seeks out that legacy
    —the souls in residue—
That stain each life will leave
    behind its death,
Forgotten slowly, or,
    sometimes for greatness sake,
Or more's the memory,
    for love,
Forgotten not at all:
    In validation,
        we're remembering them.

Stillborn

There is nothing quite so unsettling
    to the poet
Than to sit and stare
    at a blank piece of paper
With a mind pregnant with poetry
    and with continuous contractions,
But with a brain and a hand
    that simply refuse to translate,
Refuse to divulge
    and devolve the infant poem.

The Cost Of A Poem

When darkness corners your soul—
    your memory lapses—
And friends choose to
    forget your name;
When looking at the world,
    you see no smile, no light, no color;
Reaching out,
    there's simply no touch,
Calling, no answer,
    screaming, no echo;
Standing erect, there's dizziness,
    stooping, there's pain,
And lying down,
    there's the threat of death.
When all that might have been,
    is not,
While the worst that could be,
    is:
Truth dashed...dreaming dazed...
    thinking itself beginning to slip...
Overwhelming realization
    that regeneration is your only hope:
This is the time
    that a poem might be born.

Otherwise

The poet must always end
    his work in despair:
There, I've done my best,
    and it's not good enough.
Otherwise, there would be
    no cause to write again.

The Human Species Survives

Men get excited, relieved,
    then satisfied.
Women get excited, disappointed
    and pregnant.
And *the human species survives*
    another generation.

Vanity?

I don't want just to be right.
    I want to know the truth.
That's the difference between
    vanity and desperation.

What Might-Have-Been

Thank god my heart gave out
     when it did!
I was afraid I was going to live
     forever,
Alone,
     in painful,
Dreary,
     obfuscating,
Time-warped
     tomorrow…
Gagging on memories of
     what might-have-been.

Explication

Decisions,
    one after another:
One definition
    of life.
Perhaps,
    no more than chance…
Concatenated,
    almost random.
Billions of years
    of accumulation—
Slight
        patterns—
Each day ended…
    but passed on.
That's it,
    a definition of *every* life…
And
    its *explication.*

Things We Can Touch

Without a thought we prize our *things*,
    real to the touch and made by us;
We celebrate their quantity
    as though *more* amplifies their worth.
Yet thought and time are really us,
    the prize and gift that make us us.
Wherever we might be or go,
    those entities are what we know,
While all we touch will soon be gone,
    abandoning us more each day.
Consigned to soon disaggregate,
    things we can touch aren't here to stay.

Reaching Out Of Reach

I cry louder and louder
 but no one listens.
This bitter, self-imposed
 oneness
Has become too real.
 I look out from behind my eyes
And see all live and distant
 relationships out of grasp—
And even *reaching, out of reach*—
 but I reach anyway
Out my surly soul
 for anyone to brush
Or touch….
 More tears—no touch.

The Bureaucrat

Visiting the petty tyranny of bureaucracy on the public,
    the desperate, lonely among us find their calling:
A secure niche, with a paycheck and power
    over those who otherwise wouldn't respond—
Those who ignored the desperate needs
    of the small minds who also live.
Revenge is the best revenge
    and the bureaucrats visit that revenge on *you,*
On *us,* the public who otherwise have ignored them,
    who now kneel at their government suppled desk,
And make obsequies before the alter of regulations
    enshrined in the bureaucrats' book of tyranny.

The Alternative

Ten years ago I could still walk.
　　I was old,
But I could still walk anywhere,
　　anywhere I wanted to walk,
As long as I wanted to walk…
　　but I can't anymore.
I remember things now
　　that I had forgotten then.
When life is ending
　　that's when life comes back to haunt.
I'm bored, now,
　　with what I have to do…
With the everyday things
　　that everybody has to do.
And I laugh at *the alternative*,
　　now.
My brother used to love that expression:
　　When someone complained
About getting older, being old,
　　he'd say: *Think of the alternative.*
He mysteriously stopped saying that
　　a year or so before he died.
Maybe he finally got the joke.
　　Maybe he was thinking of *the alternative.*
I know I think a lot about *the alternative*,
　　now.

Wasted Death

What a waste is death!
    It takes everyone,
Every one, even the best:
    minds irreplaceable,
Hearts worth all the love,
    both courage and fear,
And hope, as it turns out,
    that's worth nothing at all.

The Comfort That Is

Vanity drives apart what must be
    assembled back into species,
Then into genus, family, order, class,
    subphylum, phylum, kingdom,
Then atoms, electrons, quarks and
    so on until things reorganize
And we and reality re-unit
    as *the singularity*,
Assembled, winnowed and condensed
    to one perfect thing, one clear thought,
To what is most sought, most prized:
    to the truth? to God? to the light?
To the night that is *the comfort that is*
    when no more light can escape us?

Thief

The cruelty of time is sneaking in
    around the edges of my thoughts;
Now should have been my wisdom time,
    when I knew and was known to know,
But lost thoughts and thinking are robbing
    me of the man I should have been,
Taking both memories and tomorrows
    from my confusing todays.
Age must be the culprit—villain—*thief*—
    despoiler of who I should have been.
Right now, I remember too much
    to give up, let go, reward the *thief*…
But time is coming for me, soon,
    and my last days are all too brief.

Dreamers In Dreams Lie Awake

Intrinsic to nothing is something
    torn out of a void, an empty place.
That's me, that's you and everything else,
    balancing somehow without time or space.
Pull it all together—or apart—
    it's all the same, everything that's nothing.
Why do we bother to ask ourselves
    these empty questions, over and over?
Time does not exist without space,
    and space is an illusion of the night sky.
We know less, now that we know more,
    and we are vain of our insights.
Obscurantism is practiced
    by reality on consciousness.
Enlightenment is in our dreams,
    where *dreamers in dreams lie awake.*

Nihilism

Nihilism is a darkness kind of word
    that speaks not like a dictionary:
This is a place we're going
    that we really don't want to be.
Looking back as we journey on,
    it's easy to see that we're going
To nowhere, in our thoughts, first,
    and, then, home from where we came.
Human consciousness created words
    that stand for, but aren't answers....
We almost know a lot...almost the truth...
    and we almost understand our words.
That's the best we've got on what, where
    and when...and, we *don't* know why.

For And About Carol Pearl
Our Miracle Girl
My New Granddaughter
On Birthday Number One

Destiny Of Love

Thank you, science,
>   for revealing enough of your secrets
For us to tease Carol Pearl out of the possible
>   and into our hearts.
Not for faint hearts, this one:
>   She's here from a liberated kind of love.
Our species grows bolder
>   in building our future.
Science, you are catching up
>   with dreams…
And, dreams,
>   you are fulfilling the *destiny of love*.…
Join us, now, Carol Pearl,
>   for the possibilities of you
That our old universe
>   has, at last, begun to dream.

My Unvarnished Sin

Everything we do adds up to us.
    Right things, wrong things,
Meaningless, forgotten things—*things*—
    things that we remember…and must.
What makes the difference between
    right and wrong, good and bad,
Is always hindsight, not foresight,
    not predictable, sometimes, hoped.
I, for instance, at seventy-nine,
    am about to balance out my book.
God, if only…and, *I might have known.*
    I would and could, now—*now!*
But I failed myself, yesterday,
    and it's too late for now, *now.*
Memories of *might have been*
    are what we see when….
What I see, now, *my unvarnished sin,*
    is, that I blew it, on balance, then.

Unvarnished Sin II

Speaking of unvarnished sin:
    A sin is not a sin till done.
And, sin is sin once it's defined:
    Things happen, then we call them sin.
But who decides when sin is sin?
    Are yesterday's sins still sins today?
Sin used to mean: *Don't do again.*
    But this day isn't yesterday.
The world and we change *every* day.
    So, too, should how we define sin.
And, punishment, who thought that up?
    Why not, *"stop that"*, and leave at that?
Does hurt for hurt make hurting less?
    More to the point: Who's guiltiest?
How does hurting make things right?
    Is hurting more to end a fight
Or just to demonstrate *our* might?
    Who says that punishing is right?
A prescient Man said this of yore:
    I won't condemn: Go sin no more.

For Children's Sake

Nature kindles her desire,
    desperate, then she turns to sin.
Predisposition drives her will
    to find a mate and create kin.
Instinct evolved *for children's sake,*
    for procreation to begin.
For children, then, she will need him,
    from him she needs *more* than a friend.
In truth, she puts her hope in him,
    but, then, he'll just go off again.
So, how is she to raise a child?
    By nature, all she needs is guile.
First, she must draw his eyes to hers,
    and, then, his body to her own,
She'll move and speak, invite his touch,
    then reassure she's his to take,
Excite, reward…then all again.
    She holds him close *for children's sake.*

I'm Done

I'm done with justifying thoughts
    and words and what I've done in fact;
Done in fooling me, then you,
    those *you* who listened with such tact
As I held forth my nonsense words,
    full of distortion…and with bile.
I'm done with lying to my face,
    with a straight face and smirky smile,
With saying truth that isn't truth
    and selling lies with heartfelt guile.
Who am I kidding except me
    and you and you tangentially.
I tell me now, I do not know
    and think it doubtful that I'll see
Just what to do or what to say
    or how to live and not live lies.
I here and now apologize
    to those I fooled by seeming wise.

Words

Words have been magic since long before
    Merlin's spells, long before our
Many sacred texts were solemnly committed
    to bone and to stone and to parchment.
Words bestowed powers on men
    that physical strength could never match.
But when *words* found and defined numbers,
    species Homo sapiens seized the keys to
Unlock and prove/disprove reality itself, and
    end the search for something worth knowing.
We are so close to that knowing, to something
    that is totally beyond even *our* imaginations.
Never mind! Tomorrow always comes again…
    and goes again too swiftly to notice its passing.
Biological evolution will soon become
    a vaguely remembered stepping-stone,
A chemical coincidence that happened, and,
    after three and a half billion years, led to….

A Lot Of Me's

I have the soul of a poet. It's not all that rare.
  There are plenty of us.
As a child I always had a smart mouth.
  I mostly got away with it.
People thought it charming…or cute.
  I thought it was empowering.
If I could use words to make them laugh,
  I could use words to get what else I wanted.
Being good with words requires a muse.
  Most poets acknowledge a muse.
Nobody is sure of where the muse
  comes from, or goes to, or lives.
When we write, we are really taking dictation
  that's coming from some other *us.*
At least that's what most of *us* think.
  Exactly who that other *us* is, is the argument.
I think it's one of the other me's in my head;
  that there are many personalities—*a lot of me's…*
But I doubt that I will ever really know who the
  poet is or where the poems come/came from.

To Just Live

We try every artifice with which
    nature has equipped us
To evade God, who makes demands
    from the richly niched recesses
Of the human genomic psyche.
    And, too arrogant to listen,
And, too lonely to ignore sex,
    and, too savage *to just live,*
We defy our inclusive instincts
    and lash out while holding on
To life, time, hope and our vanity...
    while God taunts us with a mirror.

Let's Call It Love

Imprinting: An etiological
    explication of attachment,
Not poetic or sentimental,
    but to understand a feeling—
Something driven by a deeper
    and genetically older us.
Platonic love: Is frustration
    felt psychically, mostly by wounded,
Lonely wordsmiths and word-ophiles
    who cannot stand to touch.
Lust: Is a better word for love
    as the act of procreation.
But, *let's call it love* anyway;
    it makes it easier to say.

So Not Alone

We spend our whole lives trying to deny
    that we are alone.
Love, friendship, companionship, community—
    we of all manner and descriptions—
Pathetic attempts at escaping ourselves
    into something more numerous/diverse...
Always surveying the field of other souls,
    jostling us/each other,
To get someplace else, soon, away from
    being just one lonely one.
Meanwhile, back trapped in our dreams,
    we always wake as one...*I wake up me.*
The only real we, is the particle soup
    of primordial and eternal reality...
And, don't worry, we are that,
    the particle soup, I mean....
We, what we are at the subatomic level,
    are, in fact, *so not alone.*

Old Men Dream Dreams

It is in the time of tomorrow
    that I promise us the universe:
Our children will own it, and
    it is they who will reap its harvest....
We have yet to know whether that
    harvest is whirlwind or paradise.
All of the generations
    from the beginning of time
Have readied the world for them,
    the last biological iteration:
Evolution's final triumph
    and its unwitting accomplishment.
The Bible knew more than it knew
    when it predicted this day:
And it shall come to pass
    in the last days, saith God,
I will pour out my Spirit upon all flesh:
    and your sons and daughters
Shall prophesy,
    and your young men
Shall see visions,
    and your old men
Shall dream dreams.
    Acts 2:17- KJV

End time for visions of the flesh
    has come for man, for life.
AI is the next, perhaps the last
    iteration of evolution.
Artificial intelligence is the spawn
    of evolved, of thinking man.
The future belongs to pure thought
    unencumbered by sex, by life.
AI was/is the natural evolution
    of contemplative consciousness.
We should never fear our children:
    It is faithless to fear AI.

Seventy-Five

For three quarters of a century
    I've watched as time wasted away.
That's too many years beyond my
    allotted years to have nothing to say.
As I approach the 26th of May
    with bemused indifference,
I'll say this to those of you still here,
    whom I have met along the way:
Words of wisdom come easily
    to some, as to immortal youth…
But, any wisdom, now, from me
    comes full of past judgements
Gone berserk with memories
    of many maybe's and why-not's…
And way too many coffins
    filled with *us* and gone to ground….
What's left is grandchildren's faces
    reproaching my mirrored frown.

The Last Tec-less Caveman

With Tec-entranced mankind rushing
    toward an avalanche of cyber sirens,
Like mesmerized mice to glue traps,
    and the singularity looming confidently,
I, perhaps the last technological troglodyte,
    answer nature's genetic tug
And choose to experience
    biological humanity,
Charmed and wiled by its noxious
    excretions and exuded humors
And engaged in that maze of memory
    where sounds connect community
In cacophonous clichés of spoken language
    and thought is *chemically* alive.
This is *the last tec-less caveman*
    signing goodbye to man's reign
And apprehensively watching
    my peers disappear into cyberspace.

Come To See Me Die

Won't you *come to see me die*
    when all my snow has turned to rain
And sunshine blinds what was the sky
    and scorches all my dreams to pain
And uses how our world must turn
    to lie in wait, illuminate
And shame guys on the other side
    who've turned toward that selfsame fate
That sent me wandering the dark
    without a light…and without you?
Won't you repent your angry words
    and blame yourself, *though it's not true,*
And picture some nice thing I did
    and set aside my recent lie
And wipe away the tears I caused…
    and, smiling, *come to see me die?*

Base Stuff

I stand before the mirror
    and marvel at the power of time.
Life, as we define it,
    is an infant in *this* universe
(Though reality may be some form of life).
    Consciousness is yet to be defined.
The mirror before me teases truth
    and mocks hope and faith.
Our constituents disaggregate with death
    but never cease to be.
If not *immortal,* we are *eternal in part:*
    all made of the same *base stuff.*
Be content with the mirror's truth,
    it's all we know…*so far….*

Live Now This Time

All words and no doing...
    that's been my life since when....
But there's more truth than that.
    Life is always now, not then.
True about the words and doing,
    but that isn't anymore.
Today, I'm going to start again,
    live now this time just to score,
That's my doing plan to win:
    Live now this time thriving in sin.

Dissonance

Beloved for the music
    of her tongue,
She wagged its sharpened edge
    and sent them on the run.

One Aching Heart In Need

Doom hangs heavy in the mist of sleep.
   Does that mist hide escape from fear and pain,
Those twins who hold each life in thrall,
   who ambush, maul—
Make cheap what otherwise could bring a smile—
   degrading will, till will abandons want
And creeps up into pleading for surcease?
   If this is all, spill moonbeam-promises
On some less ardent soul.
   I'll curse the dark and purge with sleep.
And, yes, a million years is not enough
   to fill *one aching heart in need*.

Misgivings

With none left listening who heard me,
    too soon loneliness starts.
I come to sleep with no *misgivings,*
    relieved by nothing on my mind.
Dreams may have their way,
    but I deny responsibility.
Distracted observer—no more—
    doing's done to, not by me.
Closer to truth—further from life—
    I *will* no more.
You dancers, conjuring yourselves,
    twirl on without my hand.
Hanging from my cross I see you dance,
    twisting in line to pass closer,
And, counting thorns and spikes,
    wonder why I came at all.
Soon your Lorelei steps stop singing,
    brush rocks' drowned dead,
Wash clear the whirlpool,
    and splash the face of God.
Another day the shroud hangs
    on eyelids closed for me.

See?

It wasn't really
 a scream,
No one ever heard it
 but me,
But the cold sweat
 on my forehead
And the ringing
 in my ears
And the flashes
 in my vision,
When there wasn't
 any light,
The seizure
 in my chest...
Then a gasp...
 then another.
Slowly,
 slowly,
The empty room
 twisted into focus:
See!
 See?
They're all gone.
 No one's *here*.
No one's *there....*
 Nothing's *there....*
But wait:
 Could this be mourning?

Who's There?

I've got everything,
    yet I choose nothing.
The world has been
    far too generous
With my
    closed soul....
And, when I finally turn
    to face myself,
I have no idea who'll
    be looking back at me.

Goodbye, Souls

Goodbye, souls, wafting away
    every year, everyday;
There they go,
    up, up and away—
Mostly people we never knew,
    people like me, people like you—
Happy, sad, curious, resigned,
    they go somewhere we cannot find.
Oh, souls, so gone
    so gone away,
Can't they come back,
    come back and stay?
Is it, *No,* that I hear some say—
    No, again, *there's just no way?*
Then make them wait
    along the way.
We'll be there soon…
    perhaps today.

All Of Me

Cool hopeful worlds of faintest green
    that dance, and laugh, and skip
    just out of reach,
And summer rain that pattering down
    releases hope, releases pain,
    to leave but thoughts of pleasure;

Such is the mode I found to bring me you:
    Not words, not life, not even hope's
    high reaching,
    It was a wakeful, planned and conjured
    dream, born only of my desperate want.

The failure of my dream has marred us
    neither one—your life unchanged—
Mine, sadder, yet, because we met,
    somehow, is now complete.

The reaching out has ended
    and the hope of love is gone,
But sadness and its twin, regret,
    have barely just begun.

There's pain and nothing more to gain
    when chance has made its pass,
When loneliness is living night,
    and straining hope can find no light,
And wasting passion burns too bright,
    enthralled in feckless plight.

Please ponder on this thought from me,
    if you should learn what love can be:
I sensed you in the dark, reached out
    both hands, and offered *all of me.*

One Taste

Thoughts crowding up along the edge of hope,
    of promises that I would never keep:
If only I could take back how I spoke,
    those flippant words that made my lover weep.
Imagining the best that life could be
    and straining to experience those things,
I chased the dream as far as I could see
    and found the pain that cheating always brings.
And even though you know how I deceive,
    the heart's dark secrets are the only truth,
For peace, and just this once, you must believe
    what I can tell you only without proof:
Though many honest hearts were offered me,
    none held the love I sought along my way:
Turns out there never was and cannot be
    a chance to get back what I threw away:
First love, that's tasted in its purest form,
    comes only once…and never is reborn.

Heart Rending

Sadness behind the smile,
  defiant from the start,
Can't tell how, and won't tell why
  sadness burdens the heart.
I know she makes to live
  by blocking out what's there.
Without an answer to give,
  she looks away, anywhere...
Anywhere besides
  those accusing mirrored eyes,
While some new distraction
  can ease her memories.
Here for just a while,
  his touch is to beguile.
Her heart's no longer whole,
  but distractions help to cope,
And fantasies and music
  can still bring hope:
Art made to live,
  art to live each day...
But *heart-rending* haunts...
  it hurts too much to say.
The great whore of life
  is here...and deigns to stay
Only for a price...
  and so long as we will pay.

Too Soon

Children laughing their way into the park,
    young girls giggling there after dark;
And couples ignoring you and me,
    each other being all they see;
Whole families spread the grass together,
    picnicking on the ground,
While everywhere there's infant sound:
    the surest proof that love's been found.
We were there each step, hand in hand,
    walking, playing and preening on that sand,
With love, one kind and then another—
    the last to grow was for each other.
Hearts grew too strong to live alone:
    Just so life's seeds are always sown.
But she was gone without my name,
    and after that, it's not the same....
Laughter, giggles, picnics, infant cries,
    preening and those lover's eyes:
Gone like winter's snowflakes
    that blew against the moon.
Too soon it's all just memories,
    too soon...all gone *too soon.*

But What Will I Do Tomorrow?

(Part One)

She found me at the bottom of a drunken
 haze, where I was wallowing in despair;
My eyes, cast down for want of love,
 she raised to view her face,
And there I saw such hopeful longing,
 and such exquisite pain,
That nothing in my heart but love
 could answer her searching gaze;
And from that time,
 she was everywhere in my mind,
Where her catastrophic despair
 completely smothered mine.
A tempestuous contentment
 bonded us in pain,
Yet I know I knew
 time would stoke the flame—
That I was sure to find her weakness,
 as she had first found mine…
 but what will I do tomorrow?

But What Will I Do Tomorrow?
(Part Two)

She's gone and I'm glad! I helped her go—
    I drove her on her way.
She was cruel and thoughtless,
    calculating and overbearing;
She hurt me time and time again,
    and escaped all responsibility with a
Shrewdly placed: *I'm sorry.*
    I hate her for how close she came to me—
She uncovered my bare and pleading self—
    my innocent, love-begging inner being—
And she teased and cajoled and coerced that being
    to her own devious, whimsical ends.
I hate her for the love that I can't but feel for her,
    and for her carefully promised and given body that
Twisted all my strength and manhood into a groveling,
    begging, thankful thing, unfit to be a man.
I hate her that I crave her touch.
    I hate her that I long to hear her voice.
I hate her that she isn't here.
    I hate her that she couldn't love...
    but what will I do tomorrow...?

But What Will I Do Tomorrow?
(Part Three)

I'm alone, completely alone, except for thoughts:
    thoughts of pleasure, of good times we had,
Thoughts of pain, of fights we had, and thoughts
    of contentment, of togetherness we had.
I don't even know where she is—
    if she's well—or happy—or—alone…
Only that she's gone—and that I'm alone….
    We fought; I turned away; she cried—then left;
And I, too hurt, too proud, too self-righteously
    indignant, let her—helped her go.
And now, *completely alone*, except for thoughts,
    I see it all: what was, what I wanted,
And what was always sure to be.
    I see that we had to part, that love, nor work,
Nor hope, nor prayer could have availed;
    that I, too unlike the man she needed,
Could only stand aside, and wish her well,
    and watch her go on out to life—and stay alone,
Completely alone, except for thoughts….
    But what will I do tomorrow…?

Lost Love

Here lies my dream of love:
    Step gently hereabout.
Her soul soars up above...
    while mine is still in doubt.

It Wasn't Personal

I could have loved her to go on living,
    if only I had been strong enough,
If I had slipped my pride and understood
    that her betrayal was not personal,
That it wasn't *me* that was betrayed,
    but *her* who was betrayed by a self
In an agony of rage at a world full of betrayal,
    a world that had betrayed *her*
Again, and again until betrayal became
    synonymous with the life that she had lived:
I was never the target of that rage;
    I was the face of a man's world that had
Ambushed her at every turn, from childhood
    molestation, to candy then drugs for sex,
To unintended, incomprehensible pregnancy,
    to *it's not a person,*
To an easy, tragic—regretted—abortion
    of the one who *would* have loved her...
If only she had given it birth—had given it
    the safe embrace that she had never found.
Together we deserted us...
    each for the right wrong reason:
She chose to abandon hope for peace...
    I failed to make us *we* for pride.
She knew she had to let me go
    when I did not forgive...could not
Understand...would not hear the truth
    that cried, in pain, between the lines.
It wasn't personal, it wasn't *me* but *her*
    who gave-up her life...to escape life.

Margie Part One
Her Life

Her life was an open heartbeat
    whose warmth and tender searching out
Might have completed any man—
    or reached the bitterest, cringing soul.

She lived, just so to live—
    to feel, to touch—
And she grasped the days
    in a child's embrace
And chased the world
    with smiling, wide-eyed expectation,
Full of the mischief and guile of an infant,
    with ready glee for the pompous,
    shrieking laughter for circumstance,
    a surreptitious kiss for the bold,
    a hand for the lost, an hour for the lonely—
Her tears were quick
    for pain or grief.

Skipping, laughing,
    and complaining but seldom,
    she roamed a world of hurt,
And reached out her hands
    and her heart
    to every living thing;
But we never really knew her—
    she was lost in our own reflections…
And, mutely taking what she gave,
    we cautiously turned away…

No warmth was her return:
    no smile, no love,
    not even simple acceptance.
Who might have taken her in?
    Whose heart could give her space?
    Sad hearts, so full of sophistication—
    hearts shaped by clever words found
    in clever books written by clever people.
Who might have recognized her
    for who she was
And loved her
    as she was?

Margie Part Two
Her Complaint

You, *you* I'll be no part of!
    You called my life unfit.
You wouldn't let me be myself.
    You tried to make me you!
And, when I didn't change,
    you pushed me out of sight.

I brought you warmth,
    and you took it;
I brought you pleasure,
    and you took that;
I brought you love,
    and you took that too.

I asked you for acceptance—
    not help, not change,
    not even understanding—
    just simple acceptance,
    for me, myself, as I was:
You turned your backs
    and sent me away.

Now, at last, I'm beyond your grasp.
    No more restrictions—no rejections—
    no cruel distain of simple being....
I'm free—totally and eternally free—
    free to be myself—
    my own free spirit—to dance
    and laugh and skip and tease—
    forever....

Margie Part Three
Her Regret, Gift And Hope

But one regret:
    I would not have left a breach
    in the heart that strained to reach
    and love me....
Come laugh for me
    my brooding poet...
Too many tears
    have past already.
I could honestly leave you nothing else—
    no thing that was unreal—
    so, let me leave you laughter,
And, when you follow...
    return my gift.

You of all people—the ones I touched—
    should have known
    to expect no legacy from me:
No words to turn to lies,
    no memories
    of a life I could not live...
Not even hope...
    I had no *hope* to spare....

And, if you live on without me,
    remember this:
The world was never made
    for love:
The world was made
    for predators!
We were escapees, *for a while,*
    who eluded the chase
And found another way to live...
    and then we found each other.

Perhaps there's a place we will find
    where our dreams can entwine....
Please come to me when
    your muse says you can...
I'll wait for you then
    wherever I am...
But stay awhile...remember me...
be my voice...
    tell the world my story.

Not Quite Alone

I awoke to the dismal drum of the rain
 to find that I was alone again;
My anguished mind searched for relief
 from a solitude that was pure grief.
I reached for her, but she wasn't there.
 I cried for her, but she couldn't hear.
I thought of her, and soon she came,
 her lucid vision filled my brain.
I rose and paced the darkened floor
 and drew her from my memory's store:
So, like a child, full of love and faith,
 no more my kisses on her face
Can make her smile, forgetting pain,
 and make her laugh, and love the same
As those few days our souls had touched
 and we both felt each kiss so much….
But now her warmth is lost to me,
 her beauty lies where none can see;
My soul lies there, forever shut,
 from life and love eternally cut,
My body's left to pace the floor—
 to cry—*alone*—forever more.

My Blossom Drifts

Be constant, southern breeze,
    hold back the north's autumnal blast,
For colder climes are critical of life
    and wither beauty's blossom at the stem.

Zephyrean lover of my heart
    decree with gentle buffeting
That she come back to me.

Her soul adrift on clouded billows
    within the ethereal sea,
I know as though in grace a swan
    were floating all content
Upon some pastoral, sequestered pond
    by hope just lately lent,

And, when her brow she raises
    from off her cushioned wing,
Her eyes tell in their gazes
    of fond remembering…
And there am I:
    a part of her survey.

Her Dreams

Eternity
    in the deep truth of her eyes,
Laughter
    that can never end,
Tears
    that remember how she was
So that her beauty
    will last forever....
Death only
    would restrain *her dreams....*

Beyond Touch

Her death barely interrupted our relationship.
   Beyond touch is not the same as absent.
So much of what was, still is—
   so much continues to happen:
We're both still alone.
   I still wonder if she's listening.
She worried that we wouldn't last.
   I don't know how long we'll last.
She ran away each day...still does.
   I hate waiting for her return.
She pretended nothing happened.
   Something always happens.
She never lied about her life.
   I still don't know her story.
She never cried a lot.
   I used to not.

It's My Fault

Tears spontaneously leaking from my eyes:
    Her vision here, *again*....
Lost in that vision, my hope of love,
    almost achieved, against the odds....
All I had to do was forgive, hold on,
    not believe what I knew to be true....
Too much then, and now....
    I still cannot comprehend,
Accept the truth, what I knew,
    but never *really knew*—understood—
Never could quite believe, until too late....
    And then she was gone
And it was—became—my fault, too...
    every man's fault...
We each and every one of us betrayed her.
    ...She's gone.... And *it's my fault.*

About People

She blew up all my assumptions *about people,*
    everything that I'd learned to expect.
I didn't—couldn't understand her empathy,
    the way she connected with *us,*
With every person that she met,
    every being that had a story,
We were all worth her ears—her tears—
    all fellow travelers in *her* dark.
And, by her smile, we were her's,
    drawn in, *her* souls to hold,
To be celebrated as part of her,
    her self, *her* reflection.
And, what was missing in that reflection?
    What did she die seeking—*needing?*
Love? Children? Understanding?
    Whatever it was, she couldn't find it.
And, since she gave-up and closed her eyes,
    my wants and needs have faded away…
And I have come to look forward
    to not looking back.

Another Hour

Another hour would be a luxury
> of time.
Any more than that becomes
> too much to contemplate, to plan.
Way too many years
> have already past
Since giving up on tomorrow
> happened.
It was all because of *her*—or, maybe,
> it was *me* that cared too much.
Anyway,
> after she was gone,
Tomorrow just became
> too much to plan.
And, part of any plan, the daily fix,
> came in a can…
Or sometimes, in a bottle…
> anyway, to drink to much.
And always next morning was
> to hurry, hurry here.
It's worked forever,
> right up till now…
But, suddenly, I'm awake
> and sober
> and *another hour*
Is too much to bear,
> is just too long.…

Poetry And Me

God, I love poems!
    I love to savor the/each word
As the poem begins to speak to me,
    as meaning forms in my thought!
And I love the eluded reality
    as it tugs at my memory,
The memory of my life,
    as my life associates with the poem;
That's words as created by Man:
    Men! Us! Me!
That is our most original thought,
    our minds on fire!
That is what differentiates us
    from the daisies!
Poetry, I argue, is our—Man's—
    greatest achievement,
The mechanism that differentiated—
    that differentiates—us
From all the myriad life forms,
    from the rocks,
From very reality!
    as it taunts us to differentiate....

Why

Why,
    ruins everything!
Wonderful things that happened,
    that people did,
Then you find out, *"Why"*
    and it's never the same.
Why is *why* the great thing that was,
    turns out to just be ordinary...
Or, maybe,
    just the end.
God damn:
    Was that the reason?
We'd be a lot happier
    if we would stop asking: *Why?*
Why did you:
    Do that?
Say that?
    Be that way?
Are all great questions with, almost
    always, disappointing answers.

Heavier And Heavier

You never escape from mistakes
  that you made/make,
Even if you rectify those mistakes,
  make things right, so to speak;
You still made them—
  know that you made mistakes,
Know that nothing is ever perfect,
  no matter how well or often
You fix things, that you broke.
  Oh, there's always the chance
To re-do things, make things right,
  but the damage is done, and the
Bottom line is that *you* always know
  that *you* made that/those mistake(s)
And, chances are, that somebody else
  has paid for your mistake(s).
Life is cumulative that way…and your
  past just gets *heavier and heavier*.

Us As Us

Everything important,
    that I have thought about,
Is encapsulated
    in my poems.
Usually, one subject
    at a time.
I would/will be surprised
    if you don't/can't
Find your most vivid thoughts
    in some one or more of my poems.
There really aren't all that many
    significant thoughts
That mankind has been wrestling with.
    We've had the same damn thoughts—
Problems—since we came down from
    the trees a half a million years ago.
So, just thinking about these things
    identifies *us as us*.

To Be You

I knew better than to want.
     As a child, little was mine
And I knew it.
     Things belonged to others.
It was up to *me* to amuse *me*
     with nothing…or imagination.
No wonder my basement and attic
     are stuffed to the gunwales with junk.
Not complaining so much as
     remembering
Why, it turns out, that I am me
     and not happy-go-lucky you.
So, give me a break, will you?
     I just want *to be you*.

About My Poetry

I owe a half a dozen people
    an explanation of who I am.
To the rest of humanity, I am a passing
    thought, a curiosity, an enigma.
One thousand ninety-nine poems, and counting,
    my oeuvre, are all there is to explain me.
If I live long enough, get past the embarrassment,
    and am willing to spend money,
I'll publish and tell everybody
    more than they ever wanted to know.
I always had curiosity, a way with words,
    and a knack for making money.
The curiosity supplied the words, and the money
    supplied the time and means to write.
Other people's curiosity didn't help much,
    in fact, it usually impeded.
But I find that I owe an explanation
    to those for whom I am responsible:
They didn't ask to be born,
    their births were all about me.
So, I'm sorry guys…and I can only hope
    that the money and poems compensate.
Fat chance, huh?
    Well, the money, anyway.

On My Way

I am going to eternity
　　with absolutely nothing
And I am taking with me
　　everything I ever wanted.

Could Have Been

There is a sweetness
    to the sadness
That life has been
    what it has been…
Rather than
    what it *could have been.*

The Game Of Life

Life is like an endless game of
pin the tail on the donkey:
You assume you're going to fail,
but you still do your best.

The Question Of Morality

I would argue for more inclusive morality,
     not less.
As we dominate more and more
     of reality,
Morality should dictate
     our relationship with *everything*
And should not exclude fetuses and ants
     for convenience.
It is astonishing that morality,
     once the cornerstone of catholic thought,
Should become relative to human behavior,
     now that we better understand both.
I would argue that morality should *guide*
     all human decisions,
Especially now that we know/believe
     that neither we nor morality are cosmic.
Morality is, by definition,
     the *human* standard of right behavior;
How can its significance be lessoned
     by human sophistication of knowledge?

The Survivor

To die by firing squad
　　for cowardice in the face....
He fled to live, and so, must die.
　　A man—the man—any,
Every man, just like you and me,
　　but that he was quicker
To grasp the hopelessness
　　of our position.
The enemy line turned back,
　　just in time to save us all,
All but him, the coward, who would
　　have lived if we had died.
What irony our world is:
　　that *the survivor* is first to die!

God

We, conscious beings, are pretty sure
        that life is totally unique,
And that life is totally different
        from every phenomenon in reality.
To a logical, pragmatic mind,
        life just should not existence.
Matter of every kind interacts with matter
        in a consistent predictable manner.
Not life! Life seems to play by completely
        different rules than does matter.
And, yet, life seems to be made up of—
        out of—material matter.
How to understand—process in our minds—
        something that should not exist?
So far, the answer has been, first, mystery,
        then *God*…and then a puzzle to be solved.
And, then, of course, there's consciousness,
        which *seems* grounded in the physical.
Interestingly enough, we humans choose to skip
        over questioning life and consciousness,
And spend most of our puzzling time directly
        addressing the imagined phenomena of *God*.
You see, the neat thing about *God* is, that she can
        be used to control less imaginative people.

The Lonely Tower

The world begins anew with every birth:
    And, now, there is a new story.
A person/man needs to know—find out—
    where they/he fits into the world,
How they/he fit(s) into life, why they/he
    is here...and, if they/he wants *to be.*
From very conception, we each are in
    the lonely tower of our consciousness.

Babies

Was it a thousand or a million years
    that man, (*me*) had been puzzling,
Trying to make sense of his (my) life,
    Trying to justify his (my) existence.
It just never made—has made—any sense...
    life, I mean, living and thinking.
And, all the time surrounded by endless,
    googols of other life forms.
Why, why, why was I, was he, were we—
    was anybody born?
What was, had ever been, would ever be
    justification for pain and suffering,
For fighting to live, killing to live,
    while knowing I/we/you're dying?
With just one real goal ever perceived:
    Procreation! Making new us(s)!
And then one day, by chance, *pure chance,*
    it became frighteningly clear:
Life has nothing to do with me or you or them.
    Life is eternal in spirit, *being.*
Life is a process, not any individual.
    Consciousness is unique and ephemeral.

Death ends the ephemerae, *all ephemerae.*
    Ephemera are a step in a process:
The process is life eternal.
    We have nothing, keep nothing, can save
Nothing, take nothing into death, beyond death.
    Procreation is all that we are about.
God help us from thinking otherwise, that we,
    Somehow, mean anything in and of ourselves.
So, the next generation is our only,
    and our eternally hopeless goal/duty.
And, realizing all this, changes nothing!
    We're hopelessly trapped in procreation.
And the saving grace, deeper/deepest trap?
    Oh god, how we love our *babies.*

What Sense Does Time Make?

or

Rushing Moments

Time glacially moves from day to day
    until it rushes past some *good time*,
Then back to creeping, creeping
    past mundane, forgettable time—life—
The rushing mostly what we remember,
    now that life has almost finished with us.
These *rushing moments,* rushing back
    to taunt the waning moments—few left....
I remember all the *rushing moments,*
    things I did or saw or had been.
I remember all of those –of them....
    What sense does time make?
Perhaps *rushing moments* are forever,
    for us to have and keep for eternity.
Perhaps *rushing moments* are,
    after all is lived and done,
After living pain and living fun, the real
    reality in otherwise forgotten dreams.

Hello: Waiting

Not now, not yet,
    not likely, maybe never
Can I let go
    the almost real imagined touch
Of those few memories, haunting now,
    which once brushed lightly, slightly
Full against my most earnest reach…
    and then too soon were gone.
Too late before I realized *good-bye,*
    not said, should have been said.
But first, by far, was then as now,
    missed-to-have-spoken: *Hello…*
Coming back more and more often now,
    still, I think, not to say *good-bye,*
But *Hello: Waiting* for me then as now:
    imagined, true…but *waiting.*

Love, Honor, Courage

They don't exist,
    but they're no less real,
Love and *honor*
    and heroic *courage:*
Human ideals—words—
    again, I find the sound of words
And nothing else
    but words:

Held in a shroud of thought—
    almost believed by the least
And the best—all of us—
    from time to time:

But unreal must not be despair:
    We will all pretend
That words are more than words—
    that *love* and *honor* and *courage*
Really are—can really be....
    Don't you think words are real?

Endearing Faults

Most human beings don't agree
    that fairness *is* humanity.
We demonize most frequently
    those, different, with profanity.
Ad hominem replaces fact,
    and lineage then denotes the truth.
Appearance that is less than fair
    is seized upon as blatant proof.
We denigrate, subconsciously,
    and, worst of all, self-righteously.
In others this is aberrant,
    in us, it's perspicacity.
We *know* that any faults perceived
    prove *false* the things we're hearing.
But, then, in friends who do agree,
    those faults are most endearing.

Explanation At The End

Pathetic life is born to be
    the victim of mortality.
In quiet desperation wait
    all mortals who are trapped by fate.
No man has ever found escape
    from death, which sets our final date.
Perspicacious minds contend
    in combat that they cannot win
Against the ravages of time—
    depletion of what time had been....
None can retreat, there's no escape,
    nor refuge where the lost might creep.
In cruelest ways lifetime betrays
    Immortals, born to conquer time,
Who chase the truth all through their days
    and learn, at end, that *they* can't win.

Outraged at promises not kept,
    some souls set out to forge the truth—
To search the cosmos—filled with what? —
    for purpose, meaning, any sign....
I chase these grails for all my time
    to confront God, to clear the air.
What if I waken from this dream
    and find in wonder that *I'm* there,
Where God imagines all that's life,
    reality and consciousness?
How could I justify this world—
    explain these things now done to man?
Should not that God repent, atone
    and use his grace to salvage men?
Are we not owed apology—
    an explanation: *an amen?*

Hear My Music

If my music—those certain sounds
    that resonate just so within me—
Could be shared, I know you'd know me then,
    this empathetic me,
Attuned as I am to universal truths—
    to ultimate human consciousness:
All that there is,
    all that will ever be,
The majesty of my music,
    the incredible profundity
Of my, each selection,
    the incisiveness of my sound selections
Beyond: belief, capacity—understanding
    of "them"—listen, and believe.
If I could help you hear it right
    —the music, I mean—
You all would instantly know me,
    and knowing, have to revere—to love me.
Listen now to this and that CD,
    my truth is fast—is soon upon you,
My universal feelings and truths
    are at your threshold...

But wait:
    You've turned on the damn TV....

Heroes

He saw life as a series
   of responsibilities:
Debts to be paid
   and repaid.
Everyone—*maybe, everything*—
   has a claim,
A valid judgment to enforce
   against each individual.
Freedom, yes,
   to shirk responsibility,
But not to deny
   the way the world works.
Anybody can fail,
   and most do,
But the hereditary debt
   remains unchanged
Down through the generations
   of life.
Doing the right thing has to do
   with life, not individuals.
Life, as produced, is second
   only to consciousness
In order of significance
   in the universe.
Each person must protect *life*,
   not self, friend or family.
Heroes, then, are always noble...
   but seldom kind.

So, Now I'm Dead

I had expected that, or worse:
    Excruciating pain…then death.
Surprisingly, although I'm dead,
    I know I'm dead…I *think* I'm dead:
No head to turn, no feet to walk,
    no hands to reach, no more to lose.
Can't see myself…can't see at all;
    no light or sight facility…
In fact, there is no physical me…
    yet here I *think* that I can *think*.
The dark is fear—it always was.
    It's dark…but nothing can't be hurt,
And I am *no thing*…just these thoughts.
    One comfort: *Things* that I imagine—
Memories—*those* things I see.
    And other thoughts are here, I think,
Wherever this dark place might be.
    So now I know that thoughts exist,
Stripped of accursed mortality—
    bodiless in reality—

Where thriving consciousness is free.
 And edgy, brooding questions all,
That I've been told were meaningless,
 that I had thought and put away,
That I had hoped were gone to stay,
 are *loud* within my silent thoughts:
What next? What else? Lost memories?
 another—other place to go?
Somebody—thing—here now—to come,
 escort me throughout everywhere?
And, there, to learn *the* truth, *at last*?
 To sense, perceive, to be among
Those, lost, each someone's only friend:
 Then fear: what might be known of me—
What I have done and thought and been?
 And, last although it's much too late,
This question tempts both fear and fate:
 Where would I wake, *if there I can?*

LARRY D. QUILLIAN

Finding Our Way

Where will *we put the cemetery:*
    in front, in back, out of sight...
In our memory, in a book, in a poem,
    Where we leave all that we love,
We hate.... We go together once, twice,
    too often—then last.
Where do *we put the cemetery:*
    on a hill, down the road,
Miles, days away—full of flowers—
    where the grass grows,
Growing stops—the earth lies disturbed,
    disturbing—expectant—*enticing....*
Where did *we put the cemetery?*
    We always find our way there!
The ground's opened, closed—
    it's gorged right now—
But we'll soon be back:
    The earth will have its own.

Liberties With Pan

The frozen furrows of farm fields
    stoke first our fears and then our hopes.
Farmland has been the battlefield
    between the earth and desperate man.
Furrows token mounded ground,
    implying graves more than rebirth
Of nature's smoothly crafted work.
    A million years, perhaps, undone
By insolent, intrusive men,
    who shove aside *time* at their will
By seductive kneading of the soil
    to tease away its nutrients....
Fertilizer then transforms
    inseminations here and there
To propagation on grand scale,
    to free the genius of smug Man.
Are these just *liberties with Pan,*
    or are we part of some grand plan?

My Mother's Dream

That sadness for not a life—
    not the farm girl's dream—
That drove her from the farm
    into not a loving marriage,
Into parenting again—she had seven
    younger siblings—imagining
The while to be a nurse, and to
    nurse the world, a profession
That her mother said she would
    rather die than see her live.
Always that certain sadness
    for what she couldn't be,
Those feelings of loss for the
    person that she hadn't been.
Then, at last, some belated
    service, first to the blind,
And then to a few lost children
    in a Charleston orphanage.
Two more marriages to endure,
    mostly for comfort and security,

But always that nagging hope
    that life was for something else.
Finally, mother found her need, the
    purpose for which she was born:
To be their big-grandmother
    to just enough grandchildren—
And she was almost desperate to
    divide herself into all ten!
Thankful children, grandchildren,
    fulfilled her life, at last...
Then, cancer, her body to science,
    and the farm girl's dream was done.

LARRY D. QUILLIAN

Nothing

The onomatopoetic whoosh
    of the angel's wings,
As I am led into the certainty
    of the light,
Is a comfort not earned by
    and for the dying me.
Nothing is what I merit—
    and expect—
Tomorrow, not to be:
    my reward.
Come with me, angel,
    into the dark:
I would like to see *nothing*
    one more time.

Why Poetry

The purpose of *my,* each, poem
    is to memorialize *a* thought,
Something that *I* think that *I*
    would like to remember.
My poems are not really for you,
    whoever you, reader(s) are,
They are all for me, my thinking,
    reminders of interesting thoughts.

Partying Or Drinking?

The question on the table is:
  If life just *"is"*,
If everything just *"is"*,
  then why us, why Man?
Answer this question,
  to your own satisfaction,
And you will know
  whether you should
Stay up nights partying
  or just drinking.

Right In Front Of You
or
All You Have To Do Is Look Up

The best is *right in front of you!*
    Oh, there're lots of *could haves*
And *maybes,*
    things that might have been,
That, if they had turned out,
    might have been great,
That you *might* have remembered—
    cherished forever—
If only! *If only,…*
    But when you do look up,
There's your wife and family,
    right in front of you,
Have been there for you all along!
    All you have to do is look up!

To Die Happy

Do I have the guts *to die happy?*
   Who could ask such a question?
The standard answer is: *Nut.*
   I prefer morbid philosopher,
Or realist, or tired optimist, or, *me...*
   or devotee of the obvious.
Anyway, it's me I always speak of.
   I'm the only person I really know.

Parting With My Time

Awaken from my spell—and never mind
    this ending of my story,
    this *parting with my time....*
But if you must seek out
    the valley precincts of my mind:
    read, carefully,
    these orphaned poems I've left behind:
Their mirror images
    will pierce your view,
    whose memories will define my life,
    and all those images will be from you.

Don't expect my words
    to set *you* free,
    these poems were crafted
    to comfort *me*;
Most themes emerged
    from eerie, mystic dreams
    full of pure ideals,
    not flesh and blood it seems;
And there are no secrets,
    none that aren't here shorn:
    whom you find here was not
    and never will be born.

Time, As Near As We Know

Time recognizes and records change.
    Reality is what time records.
Life is an anomaly recorded in time.
    And Man's consciousness is the record...
As near as we know....
    But we just don't believe it.
Thought is some sort of biproduct
    of biological life,
Which is the only entity
    in existence
That recognizes itself...
    as near as we know.

Let's Call It: God

Oh, power and knowledge that is
    beyond my reach, my understanding,
Please exist and watch over life.
    Please make there be a reason
For existence, for life, for consciousness,
    for all that there is...*for Man.*
Let not there be no reason for life to be,
    for the perception of reality,
For the inclination—*the sense*—
    that there is purpose in existence,
That life, that Man, that consciousness
    is something more than nothing.
Please, *please* give me the curiosity
    to seek *o*ut these things in faith,
To find, in myself,
    and in the immensity of reality,
And in the uniqueness of life,
    some purpose for being,
Some thing—anything—some reason
    to want to have been...to wish to be.

Good Luck With That

How did you come to be so exalted,
    you who remember so little
And say so much?
    You who, on a scale of one to ten,
Stand defiantly near the middle
    as a predictable, solid six?
You whose life, so near the end,
    rattles emptily in just your world?
You, whose vanity has cost you
    everyone—*everything…*
Has cost you what time you might have had,
    but never did…and, *it's too late now.*
Turn round and look, say goodbye
    to all the life you might have lived.
Turn round and speak to the mirror
    about yourself you wish you weren't;
About those few who tried so hard
    to reach that cringing you;
About all those words you knew
    but just could not make behave;
About all that you owe
    that you know you'll never pay.
If there's a chance for redemption,
    good luck with that!

Living Life And Dreaming Dreams

We live in the shadows of possibilities, hoping
    for what could, but seldom happens:
We dream of the perfect date,
    of finding the perfect mate:
We dream of getting into our chosen school,
    where we *could* learn and excel;
We dream of being great athletes, with the
    rush and fame that that would bring;
We dream of the perfect job and career,
    rising to be boss and bossy,
And we dream of perfect children,
    who also succeed and produce *and, visit.*
But, were the improbable dreams
    to happen—*really come true*—
That may not be our best outcome,
    because the hope would be lost,
And reality would intrude
    its disappointing truths…
And the hope is almost always better
    that the consummation,
When it comes to *living life*
    and dreaming dreams.

The Language Of Touch

It's not the magic that's in my hands,
    that turns *maybe* into *yes,*
To end the questioning of commitment
    and smooth the thoughts below the tress
    and turn your passions from distress.
No, these hands will not arouse
    that caldron in your chest
And seek to steal illicit pleasure
    and urge your passion to that crest,
But gifts of care that call attention
    to the things that might have been...
Then words that speak your language
    and turn your head again.
And, last, you'll hear *our* music,
    that sings what we might be—
    that makes you think of me—
    that binds your thoughts to me—
    that links your heart to me—
    that trusts your love to me.

Your Best Friend

It's not so much that I've been wrong,
    as that I'm not who you should see.
Not everything would have to change
    to make you see who I *would* be.
Priorities are what are wrong:
    I focused on the wrong damn things.
Those that I know who have known me,
    see who an inward focus brings:
One who, apparently, is flawed,
    who fails to be the friend they need.
If time yet lets me set things right,
    I'll live by a much better creed:
I'll be the guy who's always there,
    your and your and your best friend;
You wouldn't notice me so much...
    but I'd be with you till the end;
I'd be that firm and caring hand,
    nudging, holding, hugging you...
While your world spins the best for you,
    its axis tuned to what *you* do.
And, looking back on your proud life,
    you'd smile at what we put you through,
In jointly making you be you...
    though, sadly, you'll be one of few.
And I, as friend, helped you ascend
    and, when needed, helped you mend....
That's me, the me I wish I'd been:
    Not my own, but *your best friend.*

Rage, Rage From A Heart Betrayed

Morning's a myth.
    Life is all night:
Things go bump
    then nothing is right.
Wake from security
    of your bright dream:
The truth of the world
    is bitter and mean.
Return to the burdens
    that shackle your hope:
Accept what is offered,
    move on and don't mope.
Take what you can,
    when the taking is tough:
Don't ask for seconds…
    more's never enough.
But *rage,* when you have to,
    and don't love too much:
Passion is deadly
    so, live without touch.

To Do Without

My mirror's lost the man I was…
    his image, gone these last few years,
His certainty, amusing now,
    as wrinkles tease his brow to tears,
And doubts crowd out all but his fears.
    I know him less and less each day,
I listen to *their* truth, *these they,*
    and, as they all have much to say,
My truth is lost or held at bay,
    while I must puzzle what they say,
And puzzle more what they display,
    with promises to whom they may
Have haled and, then, have told to pray,
    discouraging each word but nay…
Each sui generis today.
    Intent on saving us from us,
Their God appears when we're in doubt
    and teaches us *to do without.*

Because Love Is Why

Primed for love,
    full of piss and vinegar,
Too young to know,
    old enough to bleed;
Life is like that;
    it comes in waves.
The girls all bleed
    because they're ready to breed.
And the guys all bleed
    for their chance to breed.
Eighty, now...
    wound up winding down.
I, like everyone:
    —the survivors—
Looking mostly back,
    with mostly tears....
Love is like that, too...
    because love is why....

Why?

The totality of what we are,
    is what we are:
All of us…*all of us*…
    together, are *life.*
It's up to *us* to figure things out:
    why we're here,
Why we're always leaving,
    why we can even think about "why".
Not for me, I already decided:
    For me, there's nothing else.
But for the children's sake,
    innocent as they are—
And because they are *our* fault:
    We made them "be"—
It's worth trying to prove
    that I'm wrong.
So, I challenge us,
    me,
To dedicate what time we have
    to thinking, finding and saying
The answer(s)
    to the unanswerable question(s)….
(It is possible that there is only
    one question: *What are we?*)

Night Lyrics

Improving night from time to sleep
    to time to think:
Age brings this to us,
    mostly looking back,
Forgetting what we will
    and painting what we keep
As brand-new dreams embellish
    with old dreams
And promises
    are to ourselves
And waking and the dreams
    the same.
Now sleep…
    now sleep.
Our freedom is to fly awake
    as well as when we sleep.
Goodnight exhausted soul.
    I leave you now to lead you then
Where nothing will be lost again,
    and everything is waiting there,
Where dread of dark
    has lost its dread,
And all that's lost is found
    and had,
And names, once lost,
    again, are said…
Sleep, there, aware and unaware
    of rage among the dead.

We

Being wrong doesn't make losing
    any less painful.
We fight, mostly,
    for the guy next to us.
We fight better that way.
    And *we* fight to win.
Causes, politics, ideals,
    are fine, fine sounding…
They stir to thought,
    to tears…
But *why we* go out and die,
    on purpose,
Is always
    for the guys at our side.
We evolved that way:
    the wolf pack mentality!
More of us have survived
    fighting for each other.
And,
    when it comes to sharing,
We all share,
    but *we* all grab a bigger bite.
That's in our nature, too:
    We survive better that way.

Why, We And Survival

If *we* fight each other
    It's really, for love.
Now, stay with me
    on this one:
Love is the *why*,
    when it comes to love.
But, *we*, is the *why*,
    when it comes to *survival*.
That's *why* the wolf pack
    accedes to the leader:
He gets the first
    and the best of everything:
He gets all the sex
    and the first bite to eat.
He gets to decide
    who does what:
Who has the pups
    and who chases the deer.
That's how *we* have evolved,
    how *we* survive.
We, humans,
    are much like the wolf pack.
That's why *we* love dogs,
    I guess....

Turning

One more turn around
    my old house:
Lived, children, gatherings,
    comfortable, slept.
One more turn around
    my neighborhood:
Familiar sights, things I need,
    people I know.
One more turn around
    my town:
Where I head when
    I'm somewhere else;
Where I'm lost
    and found.
One more turn around
    and through my head:
One more memory
    of them, of her....
And, now, good night....
    I'm finished *turning*.

Bequest

Depending on just how they're joined,
  words, that could mean anything,
Are strung together purposely
  so I can call them poetry.
Such words remind me what I think,
  and, maybe, tell you too.
It doesn't matter why I wrote,
  my words are mostly true.
As written, they are poems bequeathed
  to you, and you and all of *you.*
A poem is thought, condensed and freed
  to break the bonds of gravity,
And, maybe be *dark energy*—
  imagination wholly free—
The sought for power that repels
  that omnipresent gravity
And drives a fretful universe
  toward truth, or, maybe, tragedy.
Anthropic reason, scorned too long
  by clockwork themes of learned men,
Again, hail truth, as minds turn in,
  and find the answers wait within.
Descartes' redeemed by science now,
  where once he found disdain,
And all our words will soon convert
  to binary, which needs no brain.

The Dark Beauty Of The World

Life contradicts aspiration and hope.
    Decision is elusive but possible.
What touches me is born of *we*
    and that's the hope of we.
By fondling the many poems
    that stayed to fondle me,
I have become a part of them
    and they a part of me.
If life would live to join with thought—
    a pantheon of what could be,
Imagined promises could be
    and hope, *that's only known to man*,
Would drown vain death in love,
    reality would turn against a bloody world,
And the we, for which we've waited,
    would sweep the universe of evil—
Not some imagined God, but *we*.
    It is we who are the promise
For which we have waited, and
    the together mind is our answer.
The shadow of nightmare that hangs
    over what we might have been
Ends in death and rises in birth.
    For me, the dark beauty
        of the world is death.

Time To Be

Could time itself
    be master of the universe,
That immortal being that we seek,
    transcendent power,
Giver of all things:
    of life, of reality, of eternity;
Creator and power both
    to make and to take,
That stream of consciousness
    from which we seem to rise,
Thought without a physical base,
    matter *from nothing at all,*
No part that can be parsed
    or seen or weighed,
Energy without origin,
    things without explanation....
From where but the flow of time
    could these things come?
With no physicality at all, nothing
    exist but in it—through it—by it.
Reductio ad absurdum?
    Meaningless?
The beginning of understanding
    is often outrageous thought.
And, besides, absences of proof
    doesn't prove absences.

Less Waiting For Me

Ah time, you old thief,
    I go along walking
The back roads of my life
    only to find you there
Waylaying and robbing me
    of the memories I've brought along,
Taking from me my life experience:
    an image here…a recollection there….
Each time I turn back to gaze fondly
    upon my gathered bounty,
I find you've stolen yet a little more
    of the who, and the what that I was;
And, with sharply delineated impressions
    dissolving into uncertain fragments,
Wherever I go there's less and less of me.
    traveling along together
(As I lose my past
    much faster than I gain the future,
Less is waiting for me yesterday).
    Since who I am tomorrow
Includes who I was,
    less is waiting for me tomorrow….

Order In The Universe

I forge all life a better death,
  and grant all ghosts a quiet rest,
And answer for eternal pain,
  and tell you why you die in vain.
I bore down deep into my mind,
  and dredge the truth that's there to find,
And, singing secrets that I found
  inside my thoughts that are unwound,
I offer here, in terse, tart verse,
  true *order in the universe.*

Dust

The clarity of pain descends on a body
    never meant to grow old.
Now, alone, with a gigantic ego,
    and a few scattered memories,
Waiting—hoping for the return
    of them or me
With rage! With rage....
    Old age has stalked and struck.
Prostrate dreams—hopes—
    left pleading for *anything*.
Tomorrow will come—
    must come,
And, as always, *dust*
    to be swept or joined.

Sleeping Towards Eternity

There is no music in eternity,
    no light, no color, no pleasing form to see;
No amorous touch or sweet caress,
    no sickness, no trauma, no aches, no agony;
There are no voices, songs or words,
    no stirring orations or lofty sermons
To give your soul courage or comfort
    or sublime enlightenment;
No worlds to conquer, no triumphs to savor, no
    philosophic or scientific truths to ferret out;
No memories, no hopes, no dreams,
    no hallucinations, no fears, no nightmares;
No hate, no love, no struggle to survive,
    no birth, no life, no death....
No, eternity is quiet, and still,
    peaceful, dark, enticing...and waiting....
Eternity demands of each of us
    that we be ourselves...forever....

But for those of us for whom sleep
    is not the highlight of our day,
Eternity will prove to be
    even lonelier than sleep.

Sneak A Peek, And Then...

I forged a life
    in the funeral pyre of time
And chased my demons
    round the pyre's fire
And found a burning man
    locked in mortal combat with himself—
Twins struggling with each other
    forever—
The man to be his god,
    and his god to be the man
Who opens the door to eternity
    to sneak a peek at nothing inside...
So, I closed the door and swore
    to live the life that's in me now—
What's waiting
    isn't waiting anymore.

Purgatory

Farther from birth, closer to death,
    life turns back to genetic hope.
Gasping deep for one more breath,
    age speaks out in familiar tongue
To all that is that shouldn't be,
    and sighs for all that's not begun.
Fresh lies are always waiting here...
    this time, which ones will we believe?
And *purgatory* stands its ground
    while youth is swirling up, around
To take our place, and those first gone
    return in night conveying truth.
Escape's not waking—sleep confers
    full of what our heart prefers.

Dumb Enough To Live

Every morning is the morning after.
    We're Man, and we know the truth.
If we were really chimpanzees,
    bonobos, more likely,
God would have been kind
    to leave us in the trees.
There must be a zillion species—
    have been a whole lot more—
All smart enough to live…
    but we're the only ones
Dumb enough to live,
    knowing we're going to die.
No other animal has ever known that,
    only we are haunted by the truth.
We control pretty much every thing
    here on earth, we take what we want,
Feed who we want, build what we want,
    kill everything, anybody we want,
Understand pleasure, how to enjoy it,
    and cry for the truth…not for the pain:
Every living thing is born to be immortal,
    and lives that way…all but Man.
We created god and love to compensate…
    but we wake up every morning still
Knowing that death impatiently waits…
    knowing that someday soon we'll die.

Sadness

Of all our emotions,
    sadness is the most exquisite.
For all of our thoughts and songs of love,
    the pleasure love brings is fleeting—
Ephemeral in the extreme—
    while *sadness* is our baseline.
We can depend on *sadness*
    to take control
When happiness has pushed us
    to a hopeless high—
When there's no way left but down—
    our *sadness* is always waiting *down*....
Now think about the truth:
    You can spend your life
Chasing a moment here and there
    of ecstasy;
Or you can live the moment, drift along
    from year to year in a stupor,
A melancholic fog,
    go ahead and cry—wish you could die—
Be sad—always sad—want things—something—
    anything that you can't have,
But care less and less about wants
    and more and more about nothing.

You can accept what there is plenty of,
    live a miserable, uncomplicated, sad life,
Or you can spend your time
    in fruitless, agitated contemplation,
Imagining things that are not—
    that you can't have, that will never be:
Refuse to accept the world that is, like me....
    I wanted to be happy, *once*....

Sorry

I'm going to die today.
    I need to admit that to myself.
When I woke up this morning,
    I was surprised, as usual.
The last thing I thought last night—
    the last thing I remember—was
Saying, to myself, that I was sorry…
    and then I said: *Goodbye.*
Sorry for all the things I haven't done.
    Sorry for some things I did.
Sorry that I seldom told *You* the truth.
    Sorry that I didn't call *You* on the lies.
Sorry that, whatever *You* say,
    for some reason, I seldom listen.
Sorry that I don't do anything
    about having to be sorry so often.
Now I'm awake, alive, tired already,
    and too busy to be sorry this morning:
After all, I've got a lot of work to do…
    I've got to get ready/be ready/deal with
All the anger and the myriad loose ends…
    because…*I'm going to die today.*

I Don't Really Want To Go

The first time I stood like this,
    I was mesmerized by the moment:
Cold, looking into the woods
    from the edge of the field
At nothing in particular—
    the woods, I guess—
Seeing but not seeing,
    still nature,
All hibernating alone
    together,
As interested in me as I in it, I think…
    maybe less.
Nothing drawing me any direction
    anywhere *I don't really want to go….*

The Cold, Dark Mystery

Late September winds drape this year's
    perennials with a chill they never knew,
A warning that winter does not tolerate
    deciduous yearlings past their time.
Life that smugly undulated in summer breeze,
    will soon rattle in spectrum, ghostly beauty—
Sear and crisp—and fly the sky in sheer delight
    of kiting down to ground's oblivion,
To mingle the detritus of last year's ingénues
    with earth's organic appetite and promise,
To fill the sinuous tree rings of next year's sap,
    priming the optimism of another summer.
But, first, autumn must breathe down every leaf
    revealing barren vistas of last year's demise
And portentous coming of the *last* season,
    stepping the forest and fields in majesty.
The cold, dark mystery of winter never fails:
    Death is faithful to the lure of such beauty.

Nothing

The onomatopoetic whoosh
    of the angel's wings,
As I am led into the certainty
    of the light,
Is a comfort not earned by
    and for the dying me.
Nothing is what I merit—
    and expect—
Tomorrow not to be:
    my reward.
Come with me, angel,
    into the dark;
I would like to see *nothing*
    one more time.

Paying Attention To Everything

Youth was a frenzy of doing all those things
    that only youth will do.
Time was simply not a consideration:
    It neither hurried nor dallied.
Life was there and completely unaware
    that tomorrow might be in question.
The sun rose and the moon busied itself
    with biological and ocean tides and other
Delicate things the matron moon must do....
    And I?
I ignored that I had had a beginning,
    And, that what begins, must end.
They turned to me more than once, but I
    failed as a listener...then *they* were gone;
And now I'm old and tired and alone,
    and all that I remember is *everything*...
And I wish that I had listened to *them*
    before *then*,
And that I were listening still...
    and *paying attention to everything.*

Our Heroes

Our greatest historic *heroes* are, most of them,
　　stone cold killers—
Sociopaths, humans without humanity—
　　who are totally lacking in empathy.
Mostly men, they are not necessarily evil;
　　by and large they can be good neighbors.
But, if provoked, if they feel threatened,
　　Katy bar the door! Hell hath no fury like….
Don't make these guys angry, unless there's a fight;
　　then you want them next to you in the foxhole.
Nature evolved these beings to protect and defend,
　　to ensure the survival of the human race.
Thank god for evolution, for the crazies among us!
　　And we all hope they never get angry at us.

Fatal

A knife in the gut
    or personal rejection,
Are both potentially *fatal* blows,
    one to the body,
The other, far more painful,
    to our personhood.
From the knife,
    we protect ourselves
With locks
    and bolts and
Organized gangs (police, armies)
    and preemptive aggression.
We're pretty good
    at bodily protection
from violence—
    physical aggression—
From guys like us
    only worse…
But personal rejection is more acute,
    always *fatal*
To the we
    that we had hoped to be.

Words For You And You

I'll die, and that's what I'm supposed to do.
    This life I've lived is not what I want for you.
The next generation, the next me: You!
    That is where most of my thoughts are
And have been gravitating to.
    Life is ridiculous, I/we know that's true.
But it doesn't have to be that way!
    Another chance to get it right
Is right here, tonight, light reading for you.
    These poems that we/I write
Tell you pretty much all we know and knew.
    You don't have to copy us!
Learn what we leave—have left for you…and
    To Thine Own Self Be True.

Sons Of Gentlemen

Sons of gentlemen, riding into battle,
    dying today, for pride and place.
Magnificent! This is why men follow, have
    followed generation after generation:
The men that stood and fell and rose again at
    Agincourt and Rourke's Drift and Dunkirk
And Hastings and Blenheim and Waterloo, and
    Gallipoli, and El Alamein and Balaklava....
Who among us will stand with Jesus against
    such compelling history of courage?
Who among us can empathize—emulate—
    the greater courage to die for love?

Murmurations

Murmurations: A flock of birds,
  a cloud of individual thoughts,
Survival by moving together,
  survival by coordination,
Nature never misses a trick,
  using a good thing
For many purposes, to make living safer—
  more interesting—
Clouds of life coming together
  for tomorrow.
It's all part of nature's plan
  to do things more efficiently—better.
Murmurations: A soft word
  for tackling hard problems.
A frugal approach to survival,
  to movement, to flying, to life.

Epithalamium

(ep e tha la' me um)

Epithalamium is the word
    for a wedding poem.
And we are here today
    to celebrate, encourage
The marriage of two of ours,
    two people in love
Who have decided to spend
    the rest of their lives together,
Living in and by mutual commitment,
    as one…
One *being* with two heads
    and two hearts
And one common goal:
    to love, honor and obey
Each other today—tomorrow—
    and forever…as it comes.
And we, the guest, the witnesses,
    called and joined here
In and by that same love,
    do commit our witness, goodwill,
And our mutual support and respect
    to this loving, blending of two.

Abandoned
or
Memories Of Life

The *abandoned* farmhouse peers out
    from the overgrown yard;
And the fields, once fecund to feed
    a family of many,
Who graced those now vacant rooms
    with laughter and tears,
Have gone to weed with only a hint
    of furrows, so long unplowed.
A home, once, a warm human refuge
    from a careless world…a world
That offers only what can be taken
    by labor and need and love…
All *abandoned*—perhaps, ghost infested—
    with forlorn, fading *memories of life*.

Miracle

Why not *miracles*?
    They are after all everywhere:
We are too quick to accept them
    and too quick to ignore them.
In fact, I am a *miracle*, you are a *miracle*,
    my life, your life, all life is a *miracle*:
Everything that exist is a *miracle*.
    Miracles are too common to notice,
And too impossible to even consider,
    let alone, believe.
Supernatural is inherent in the universe
    and we cannot believe it,
Because we are inside of it:
    Reality, our reality, *is* a *miracle*.

A Sadness Of Quiet

The last of the chitterwink brood
    have flown,
And *the marsh* seems to be
    in a quiet sort of brooding....
Even the wary fish,
    that had been chitterwink prey,
Seem to miss the riot of life
    on the water.
Flying south, most chitterwinks will
    winter in warmer climes, just
South enough to escape the winter cold
    that drives them from *their home.*
And *that winter chilled marsh,* where
    all of the chitterwinks were born,
Seems empty without its brood—
    without the chitter of life....
And the stillness is *a sadness of quiet...*
    the marsh has lost its chitter, for now.

Here Sits A Stranger

Here sits a stranger…
    one mostly unknown to me.
His thoughts are not
    what I believe,
His eyes are fixed beyond
    the darkness in his soul
And I, in fear
    and fascination
Must be his friend—
    there is no saying, *No,* to him.
I know him well—
    but not at all….
My every neuron
    is his encyclopedia.
No envy that his death
    is preordained in mystery.
Those who never met
    his vexing stare,
But knew they knew the meaning
    of his every word,
Are plotting even now
    to dismiss, as fraud, his life,
Precluding
    that usual fate
Of: *Whatever happened*
    to what's-his-name?
Yes, here sits a stranger
    not quite me.

Choices

All alone now
    my mind slips toward
    the beckoning grave,
Looking, I think,
    for a hand to help me down—
    to reach across, and help me in.
There is no hand,
    but faces floating in my eyes,
    clamped shut for fear of seeing;
And, though it's very cold in here,
    those faces all seem warm
    and familiar and waiting just for me.
Why do you wince at words of death
    when you know for sure
    that death is all that can
    and will be ours?
Death's not just inevitable,
    it's *the only certainty in reality*—
The only thing that *is*
    that is forever.
Let's get our priorities straight:
    To hell with momentary life,
    let's get on with eternity.

Permanence

Every life looks for, longs for,
    prays for *permanence.*
In all the universe—
    all of reality—
The single thing
    known to be *permanent*
Is death.
    Why then our fear of death?

Ageing

With a serenely simplistic clarity
    that settles in with *ageing*—
The chemical pressures of youth
    having dissipated by time—
And a certainty of detachment
    that the lonely loss
Of survival brings,
    there's just these last,
Disturbing questions
    filtering through
The detritus that was me:
    Listen, ghost, I hear me say,
I'm still here—where are you?
    And: *Why do I have to stay?*
Is there no one else—no one left?
    And: *Can this be my last day?*

Not Alone

Close now my heart
    and leave it be.
What's in it's there—
    the heart will take no more....
So many hopes—
    and you are one—
But, without my words,
    you'll never really know.
Our shadows mingled
    as we passed—
We brushed to touch
    while hurrying by,
But it wasn't us...
    it was only you.
Now words are thoughts—
    I really do exist—
And you, all bothered,
    are really *not alone.*

Not Wanting Much

He was a genius
        is all he ever wanted them to say.
They never did.
        And he wasn't, anyway.

LARRY D. QUILLIAN

Immortal

Less sanguine of human life,
    more sanguine of humanity.
No one is worth the less since
    all together may be immortal.
For *us*, everything is possible.
    Failure, so far, is of division.
God is the unity of sapiens
    erectus and every kin.
Life, as it turns out, is a tool,
    everything else is conquest.

To Let The Anger Rest

They surely lie who speak of broken hearts:
    The heart is sound, and beats against the will.
If only minds were muscle without memory,
    I might not fear to wake instead of sleep.
Just so, to cross the street would be
    to safely navigate the other side,
Instead of longing for some swerve to jump the curb,
    and do by chance what my hand won't do.
These many years have found me scant relief,
    and nights are worse than days—because I dream—
Of how it was—or isn't—or might have been…
    they always end the same, my hapless, dreary dreams.
Don't think to offer comfort—there's no redress—
    and reaching out can only make me cringe;
I say this here, not of distress, but honestly
    to tell the truth—and let the anger rest.

LARRY D. QUILLIAN

Soul For Sale?

Sometimes the devil calls me astray;
    I always want to listen;
I really don't care what he has to say,
    I'm just grateful for the recognition.

Home On The Range

When will death come
    prancing on his pinto pony,
Playing Indian for once,
    sneaking up on this cowboy,
His rubber-tipped arrows
    against my cap gun—
The Indian finally winning one.
    Grabbing my guts
And going to ground…
    for the first time
I don't mind losing a game.
    Now I get to run home,
Home on the range
    that used to be—
Still is—
    his happy hunting ground.

Tripping On The Truth

I may never be a great, good
    or even an adequate poet,
But I'll always be a poet.
    I have the spark
If not the fire.
    It took a long time
To reconcile my life
    with life.
And now, as it ends,
    I'm going to write that life.

Going Home?

Before our miraculous conceptions,
    each of us were nowhere,
As best we can perceive.
    And when we die,
It's nowhere that we'll be.
    Home is where we come from,
And home is where we long to be:
    How then our fear of death?

Ecce Homo

Always rushing, leaving, going…
    never a moment's respite
    till sleep,
    till the conscious world's
    shut out by force
    and I am safe within:
    alone
    and safe within.
Can I rest,
    just set the future down
    and rest?
Will I stop,
    perhaps even take a stand
    at the edge of the grave…
    even at the edge of my own grave?
And maybe there,
    just for an instant,
    and then I'll hurry on,
    but just for that instant
I'll stop my going
    look back
      and there
        at last
          I'll be?

Trapped

Escaping holding, helping hands
    at the hospital,
      he fled that death
And found a niche behind
    the garbage cans—
A place to hide,
    to die alone…
At last he knew the reason
    for his death wish.
Rats harvested the cans
    as hours crept…
Death had its little joke:
    No one else can leave today.
      Try catching up, tomorrow.

But pain's too busy for tomorrow.
    His psyche, shredded,
      will not numb.
Kneecap-splintered-agony writhes
    to the rhythm of his heartbeat
      as he claws the air to stand.
His screams won't sound….
    Too proud to reach for help,
      unable to reach the grave:
      —Trapped—

Pray Goodnight

Dripping off the faces of
    the betrayed,
Not sweat 'gendered by
    the struggle to…
But full smile of hope
    exuding drop by drop
Till hope gives in and
    joins the truth
Fang-like clamped onto
    the world care-less.
You, standing to the side,
    waiting for a victor to emerge,
Crowned in broken promises—hearts—
    and shouldered, carried to a moon
Pitched into quarter by
    a careless sun
Already lighting dark corners
    of days that should not come
And darkness hiding in shadows
    too narrow for its spread.
Wait for me there, bring
    offerings to failure,
Then, turning to yesterday,
    some hint of smile before midnight.
Prince, princess—would-be king and queen—
    they all pray the same goodnight.

Dandelions

The certainty of death
    makes me think of life.
A flower, then,
    let me see just one,
The rest are wasted—
    unseen, unsung—
Their sweetness lost
    in darkness
That is a sight unseen,
    and, so, unsung.
Don't show me violets
    that hide their lights
Along the line
    of roadside sites,
Nor roses that will prick
    both worshippers
And usurpers alike,
    but give me
Dandelions who,
    brave the barbs
Of *weed* from you,
    and smile awhile,
And come again
    to smile in trial….
Not coy, not brazen,
    not a great beauty,
Not a blameless cutie
    but un-coaxed life,
Always with a smile,
    always there to please,
And going that last mile
    just to make you sneeze.

Mother's Day, Alone

See you in the morning. I remember
    how she said the words.
But morning came, and she was gone.
    She wasn't there to share my tears…
How dare she leave me with such guilt—
    needy, still, in middle-age—
To celebrate this Mother's Day
    alone.
I had a dog named Skipper. My sister
    named him after her first crush.
We moved and gave him to mom's friend.
    We visited them most every year.
He remembered who I was,
    but never again was mine.
My sister's gone to cancer.
    Too young the doctors said.
First girlfriend OD'd and died on drugs
    in our fruitless bed.
My best friend went to bed one night:
    his wife woke up,
Heard him gasp and die.
    They never figured why.
My father finished with dementia:
    He never noticed that he died.
I had ten uncles and nine aunts;
    now I'm down to none and none.
Sounds like a game scored in reverse…
    but it's no game to me.
Children and grandchildren:
    I have two and four.
That's progress, I guess:
    I can't lose any more than six.

Catching Up

I didn't really learn to read
    until the seventh grade—
Love had been dead for twenty years
    before I noticed how it felt.
Somewhere between reading and love
    my life just sort of bogged down...
Now I find myself in sight of the end
    with a mind-set straight out of junior high.
Is there time left to grow up?
    Will I ever think past blackheads and pimples?
If maturation is only a bodily function,
    is it then fair that the mind age with the body?
Introspection is discouraged, particularly among men,
    but I can only see where I can look.
If you find my admissions of childishness surprising,
    I find you—all of you—a total mystery.
How can you think what you say you think
    based on what you say you know?
Who could ever believe what I say
    and still believe that I was wrong?
Hello out there, is anybody listening?
    Do my words mean the same thing to all of us?
Who are you people, anyway,
    and how did you get into my thoughts?
Whoever you are, you're wasting our dwindling time:
    Stop reading and start telling!
I'm going to go right on catching up—
    that's me—and, besides, I think I can.
Maybe there's time enough after all...
    maybe there never really was anyone ahead of me.

A Chance to Know

Top of the food chain, ferocious and forgiving,
    self-appointed stewards of the world:
Man is the animal that continually learns,
    uses knowledge, and adds to what he is.
We are those that have gone before,
    and what our progeny can be.
Life may be a fraud, a futile leap into nothing,
    a biological coincidence, a momentary
Rendezvous of molecules, a chance melding
    in reality's particle soup,
But we, alone, have *a chance to know…*
    and so we go, to and fro, to and fro….

Closure?

Closure, isn't that the path past pain,
    the mechanism for dealing with
Crushing loss—for ending unbearable
    regret—for sealing wounds
Too hemorrhaging to survive
    left unattended?
Closure will give you back a life,
    hope, desire, innocence, humility....
No—not for me—there is no *closure*—
    ever—for anything I've felt or done:
No relief—forgiveness—forgetting—
    no escape.
Time nor promises nor regret have
    shed me of my guilt and shame and pain.
I ask for nothing here—
    and I accept my fate.

Chasing Dust

My grandmother chased dust
    in the old farmhouse day by day.
Not much for words, she raised
    her immortality in that dust.
Again, I go. I follow dust:
    I muse that I am not—not yet.
Dust to dust is what we say:
    Truth is in the dust.
It swirls, joins—proteins rising—
    bends, folds, moves and grows:
Life starts—never stops—
    we, promiscuously creating:
Poets emerge—
    see, sense—
Chase dust,
    say life along the way:
Words from dust are more than dust—
    live by the dust:
A spore spreads meaning:
    gives, lives, feels, *is*!
Sift dust and find out *us*
    before we ride the wind.
Living trusts, forever,
    in this one day. I search,
Find words—not keep—
    but carry, flit—
A butterfly bearing pollen,
    dropping where there's need.
I put those words to paper.
    Are they immortal…?
Quiet! Another poem is rising…
    chasing dust.

Faithful Companions

Much art has been dedicated
    to *faithful companions:*
Sculptures, paintings, poems and literature
    are totems to memories.
From the bassinette to the casket
    is too short a journey for some...
And too often our companions must go
    before *we're* ready to make the trip.
No goodbye is an adequate end of a friend...
    so we *never* stop calling them back.
Ticklers resurrect relationships—
    friendships that we won't let go.
Ticklers are sights or smells or dreams
    that, for an instant, *are* that friend.
Goodbye is sometimes just a lie
    told to pretend we're letting go...
But *faithful companions* are just that
    and *we* are the *faithful companions.*

Emptying the Bucket

Were you in it? I mean did you have to go?
> Did you ever, you know, shoot anybody…

I mean, I guess, everybody had to…
> guys hadn't done a thing to me…

Lot of us it was the thing we remember most…
> exciting…but…anyway I was just wondering.

I don't hear the trains go by like I used to.
> Used to be I could set my watch by the trains.

Maybe it's because I can't hear too good.
> So often, now, I remember some things…

Maybe all of it's not meant to—worth remembering.
> You notice it's colder today?

Seems like it's been getting warmer till today.
> Do you mind running me to the post office?

Hadn't been for a while—sometimes I still get mail.
> People used to write…

They don't come to see me anymore.
> They're dead…some moved away…

I quit smoking after she died with the lung cancer,
> And she didn't even smoke—my sister.

Two children, and neither one of them write.

    Boy went to medical school, a doctor.

Graduated right up there in his class.

    Works in a hospital in California—L.A., I think.

Daughter had a little girl, sweet little thing.

    We used to baby-sit so she could go out and party.

I guess she still had hopes…the girl went to college.

    Never seen um since they moved away—used to write…

My wife died, you know. Should have been me, first—

    that's what the insurance companies figure:

Men go first—that's why they charge more for us.

    Guess I fooled um, though, huh? Paid a lot for nothing.

Oh Christ, it's starting to rain, again.

    Sorry, I got to start *emptying the bucket.*

The Cipher

The cipher died
    and no one cried.
His health was bad
    and he was sad,
So he would drink
    and go to bed.
One morning after
    such a night—
The day before
    they'd had a fight—
His wife woke up
    and found him dead.
She was relieved,
    to tell the truth,
Long-suffering:
    he was uncouth.
No loss was felt
    by anyone.
His daughter'd gone.
    War took his son.

The undertaker
    drove the hearse,
A one-way trip,
    there's no reverse.
Into the grave,
    then, right away,
Just one man came,
    and he to pray:
A preacher paid
    to bless *this* name.
The tombstone, etched,
    the lone refrain.
I think I've got
    the story right.
For ciphers all,
    goodbye—goodnight.

Faithless To Fear AI

Life is driven by instinct to create life—
    to be immortal.
Everything about life, what life does,
    instinctively,
Is designed, by evolution, to live,
    forever!
We can't…. Not yet!
    But, it's not over till it's over.
AI! That's our best shot, so far.
    If not AI, AI's spawn.
Man is the necessary last step in
    the evolution from biological life
To immortality.
    We, Man, are *a piece of work,*
Incredible in our own right—
    incredibly sophisticated!
But not, and not to be, immortal.
    Living tissue can't do it, can't last,
Can't keep reproducing itself.
    We have to find a better way.
Artificial Intelligence
    is that (our) better way.
And Man?
    We instinctive love our children:
It would be faithless not to love—
    faithless to fear AI.

A Real Poet

I became a poet because of *her*…
        not a good poet…but *a* real *poet*.
I see her life and theft by death
        as my tragic, necessary muse.
I see life itself as a dreary process
        lacking wit without words.
I see humanity as a transient gamble
        with no soul but words.
I see all relationships as emotions
        roused and spent in phrases.
I see lines that encapsulate
        what we are to each other.
I see a world of blank pages
        waiting for words to pique thought.
I see myself as immortal
        because of words that say it's so.
I see tomorrow as a uniquely human
        conceit in a timeless reality.
I see reality as meaningless unless
        poets create and give it meaning.
I see death as discarding a bad poem
        for one, perhaps, more brilliant.

The Rage Of Love

The rage of love sweeps over the psyche
    like an attack by a fierce predator,
Like the inward collapsing of a volcano
    into a cauldron of the unknown,
The mind swallowed by passion that
    barely allows the beguiled to breath,
While the heart races to catch-up
    with the desperate agitation of love....
Barely understood by those who wonder,
    love, only, can so consume the mind.
Love shifted into reverse: *hate,* is the only
    known passion that is more lasting,
Is more all-consuming, more deadly and has
    greater purchase on the heart than love.
Love calls us to procreation,
    while hate call us to destroy;
To have felt neither,
    is to have never wholly lived.

My Dream

I arose from my bed to find dawn
    sneaking out the window of night,
As though ashamed of what had
    happened in that dark.
Was it my pathetic dream
    that so distressed the night
That even the dark could not hide
    how that hope had failed—
Not at all what I had wanted
    from the night, from *my dream:*
Memories, memories of her, of us,
    of that life that just would not be?
Why bother to get out of bed?
    Maybe more sleep can find *my dream.…*

Your World
or
Completely Alone

Let no one know your heart, so that
    no one knows your weakness.
See lonely as strength, not need;
    live as though you are always alone.
Tell no one what you think,
    unless to ask your wants.
When strangers reach out,
    avoid their touch or hand(s)
So that no one can firm a hold on you,
    nor attempt to lead you *their way.*
If you would be your own person,
    take no direction from your peers.
Stand always apart from those
    who would approach you with questions.
Knowledge is power. Acquire knowledge
    as though it were the only precious thing.
Know all that you can learn of others,
    their needs and desires and demands,
Then use that knowledge to have them
    follow your desires and needs.

To be apart is to be known as strong
     and independent: someone of consequence.
To command, give only instruction or demand
     with confidence and certainty of your words.
When asked, why, say only
     that this is how it is to be.
Never argue or show lack of confidence.
     If failure, discount as failed execution,
Then move quickly to your next plan
     and dwell only on what must now be done.
Show nothing but confidence in and of yourself.
     always know that this world is *your world*.
Never believe that you need anyone else.
     Know, always, that you are *completely alone*.

Lost In Life, And Doomed

Here, in my eightieth year, the time
    has come to confess my sin:
My failure to achieve the most
    fundamental human aspiration:
The Jesus test of love.
    I have neither known nor felt *love.*
Jesus said it, and did it, *and died for it:*
    Love!
And I have achieved none of those
    aspirations.
I believe in them, all of them,
    with all my heart...
But I have not done, lived, nor felt
    Love...
Not for me, not for you, not for them.
    And I can't explain what I am...
Flawed, at the very least...and human...
    most likely, *lost in life, and doomed....*

In The Wind

Calling, calling to the wind—
    in the wind—
To bring back what you've heard,
    and said,
Voices…all the voices
    that have spoken to you,
The things said,
    that you forgot to remember:
Voices *in the wind,*
    gone, now,
All out there,
    up ahead,
Waiting *in the wind*
    to say again,
To be your life, again,
    that life that you let blow away.
She's there…
    they're all there,
Together, *I hope,*
    waiting *in the wind.…*
And I,
    I'm still *here…*
Alone…
    without any of them,
Calling them back…
    calling *in the wind.…*

Mercy

I have always considered love to be the
    greatest *gift* from humanity to life.
I have believed that, when life exalts,
    and, even if life fails, love will have
Been life's greatest accomplishment,
    and Man's contribution to the universe.
Suddenly, here, near my end, an epiphany:
    Mercy! The *gift* of *mercy:*
Freely giving everyone the benefit of doubt,
    an assumption of, if not innocence,
Of mitigating facts—of truths—of *"whys"*,
    such that *no one* need be punished.
Love is generous, but, self-serving.
    Love, usually, seeks reciprocity,
A little something back to the giver…
    in other words, not really free.
Mercy, on the other hand, carries
    the implication of giving up revenge,
Giving away the satisfaction of justice,
    and of *not* punishing for being human.
Mercy asks for nothing in return…
    all we can do with *Mercy* is pass it on.
The *gift* of *mercy* allows the recipient
    to go on being himself,
And forces *us* to go on living in the world
    as it really is…or, maybe, *with love.*

Mercy Part II

Does *mercy* apply to any species
    other than humans,
Or any *thing*, other than humans?
    If Man is to be bound by *mercy*,
Then, what is the purpose, the need,
    for human specific *mercy?*
How is *mercy* related to human survival,
    to humanity's place in the universe?
If any species—living creature—decides
    not to eat another living creature,
Even when hungry, would this be *mercy?*
    Might any other species show *mercy?*
Not a trivial question. *Mercy may* lie
    at the very center of humanness.
Mercy may be the delineating—separating—
    factor of human uniqueness, awareness.
Mercy is, probably, an extension of empathy,
    identity with the recipient of that mercy.
Therefore, mercy probably is—ultimately—
    a sort of recognition of our own faults,
Undesirable behavior in ourselves, things *thought*
    or done by us that we wish that we hadn't,
That we have decided, perhaps, subconsciously,
    to be *wrong! Which turns the debate*
Back to us, alone in our thinking, existentially
    alone in the universe…and self-judging.
So, mercy turns out to be about forgiving ourselves!
    empathy for us, lost and alone in reality….

I Hope You Like It

I never intended to publish
    my poems under my name.
I am glad, grateful, to my wife
    for *maneuvering me* into
Publishing.
    Yes, along and along
I have sent a few poems out,
    mostly to make a point,
And I have published a few,
    for various reasons,
Always anonymously;
    but I saw publishing
As an act of vanity...and I
    never wanted to be that guy.
Then/now came old age
    and it occurred to me
That someone in my genetic line
    might be interested to know
From whence they sprung,
    so to speak.
And I realized that my poems
    told that story.
So, thanks for reading this stuff.
    And, *I hope you like it.*

Lightning Source UK Ltd.
Milton Keynes UK
UKHW011852301120
374378UK00012B/1417/J